Reflections of Cork

AN INSIGHT INTO CORK LIFE / BY CORK PEOPLE

Reflections of Cork

AN INSIGHT INTO CORK LIFE / BY CORK PEOPLE

BY PAUL DALY   PICTURES RICHARD MILLS

Evening Echo

a Thomas Crosbie Holdings Ltd. Company

Published 2004
by Evening Echo Publications
a Thomas Crosbie Holdings Ltd. Company

ISBN
0-9528856-4-6

Design and layout by Edward Butt,
Graphic Artist, Examiner Publications.

Printed by City Print, Victoria Cross, Cork, Ireland.

Kieran Cotter

"It was the weekend after the August weekend, so the village was very quiet. Wintry, windy, showery. The weather was unsociable.

We were actually called out by some photographers from the Examiner, I think it was. They had chartered a boat from Schull and hadn't returned, so there were some concerns. They didn't know if they were safe, because they couldn't contact them. You know, communications weren't as good that time. Some boats had VHF radios alright, but there was no such thing as mobile phones.

So we went out looking for them initially and after we couldn't find them, we pulled into Cape Clear and made a couple of phone calls. We discovered that they had arrived back safely in Schull and while we were checking that out, we got a call to say that a yacht called Regardless was in difficulty four miles south east of the Fastnet. So, we went out to her. And the big problem was to find her.

The navy ship was out there, and there was lights everywhere, high wind. The chaos was really created by boats being everywhere. If there only had been one boat out there, the situation wouldn't have been so chaotic, even though the winds were very strong.

The lifeboat we had at the time, the machinery, the equipment, wouldn't be half as manoeuverable or powerful as the one we have now. At that time, we didn't have a VHF direction finder, so we could talk to them on the radio, but we couldn't identify where they were. Today, you talk on the radio and you get a bearing, and you can head directly for them. Eventually we found her and towed her into Baltimore.

Was I scared? Not really, no. Young people don't get scared anyway. What about the fella going down the road at 120 miles an hour on a motorbike: is he scared? That doesn't really come into it I think.

Charlie Haughey was September 1985. His boat hit the rocks, for one reason or another, off the Mizen. At first, we didn't know who we had; there was just five people. One in a dinghy and four in a liferaft. They were north of the Mizen in a sheltered little cove. Mind you, they were extremely lucky to get out alive. And they were aboard about 15 or 20 minutes before someone decided, 'He looks very familiar.' It was my brother actually who recognised him and who wished him a belated 60th birthday. So we brought him in and there was the height of publicity.

Fastnet Race was an exception, and Charlie Haughey was an exception in terms of, there were five people in a dinghy and one of them turned out to be very famous. Normally, you get simple calls: just people breaking down or having small problems. In the summertime, we get a lot more calls, because lots more people are in the water. In the winter, most of the people in the water are professionals. Professional people usually have good equipment and are dealing with the whole show in a professional manner.

What's happening today, people are buying boats. They know nothing about the sea. They aren't properly trained, they haven't got the proper equipment and they don't know what they're doing. They don't know how to use it properly and, for one reason or another, things start to go wrong and they call up and say they have a problem. Quite a lot of it is just lack of knowledge. A lot of calls we have are just easy calls to deal with."

Kieran Cotter is a shopkeeper. Originally from Cape Clear, he spent a number of years at sea before moving to Baltimore in 1977 to run a shop in the village. The 49 year-old lives above the store with his wife, Brigid, and their three children.

He celebrates 30 years as a crew member of the Baltimore lifeboat in January 2005. He is the only current crew member who served at the time of the Fastnet Race in 1979. He has been coxswain since 1989.

Claire Nash

"My name's spelled C-L-A-I-R-E. The French way. You'd wonder whether I was conceived in France or something, but I wasn't. I was conceived in Abbeyfeale in my godfather's hotel.

I suppose Ballymaloe started my passion for the industry that I am in. I got a job from Myrtle Allen when I was thirteen, having said I was fifteen. In those days you got away with it. And she literally taught me how to cook. I ended up going to the States when I qualified.

I just decided, 'I'm going to come home and I'm going to open something.' Number one, I hadn't a bob and there's nothing to drive you on like the old pinch in the pocket! We'd had a family tragedy: I had to come home, end of story. I was the only one in the family who could really come in and fill the boots at the time.

So I opened Nash 19 – a little institution – in 1991 or 1992. I started with 12 staff – we now have 24 – and we do what we do. We do it well – we try to do it well. We open at 7:30 and we close at 4:30 – and we've our money made: we're not greedy – and we're gone.

You need to come in here in the middle of the day. There's a great old buzz here: it's a great spot. And the day that I don't enjoy it, I'll sell it. When I start an employee here, I hire personality. I'm not too pushed that they're, 'I've worked here, I've worked there.' You'll then spend the next six months trying to beat the bad habits out of them! Service is the fifth wheel of this well-oiled machine. But the only thing that will make a person come in here every day – and some of my customers come in twice or three times a day – is the bit of service, the bit of banter. But there's a very fine line between good service and over the top: they don't want a slap on the back; they don't want a waitress sitting on their lap; but they do want to be looked after. And the day that they're in here in a professional capacity, with a colleague, a judge, their litigation lawyer, their boss – whoever they're with, whatever it is – they want to give that unsaid look to me: 'I need to be looked after today.' And we'll spot that a mile off.

If you look after your staff you'll get it back tenfold. We'd have customers that would be trying to wind up my girls against me, you know? The minimum wage rate went up three years ago. These three biddies called Mary over and said, 'See that? I bet yer wan doesn't give you that!' And Mary goes, 'Wha'? What's that? I wouldn't get out of bed for it!'

But you know, I won't ask you do to something that I wouldn't do myself. I mean, I will be on my knees scrubbing this place, I will be cleaning the toilet. You can't expect staff to work with you in front of the general public if you haven't that kind of rapport with them. You must earn your respect."

Claire Nash is proprietor of Nash 19, one of Cork's most popular restaurants, which is located in Princes Street. A native of Co. Limerick, she trained in Ireland and the United States in the catering industry. Living in Kinsale she is a keen swimmer and runner.

Conal Creedon

"A city of steps, steep hills, more steps and steeples. Where above the heads of the merchant paupers and princes, the golden fish on Shandon, casts a sceptical eye over the fish bowl that is Cork.

Two channels of the river Lee insulate the city centre from generations of Northside/Southside rivalry. Two factions holding up mirrors to each other, reflecting identical topography with carbon-copy monasteries, breweries, cathedrals, towers and bridges.

We don't call it the inner city here in Cork, it's just plain Downtown. And home for me, is a spaghetti bowl of streets centring on the one called Devonshire. My family have lived and traded here since the Vikings – a busy little shop, more social than commercial; and bivouacked in various nooks and crannies throughout the house could be found my parents, 12 siblings, a clatter of pets, and a string of guests who came to dinner and stayed.

Outside, the streets were bustling too, with families talking and taking air. Thirteen-a-side football on the street, where every boy, girl, dog and cat chased like coursing greyhounds.
Shawl-wrapped Annie selling fruit on Carroll's Quay, Connie the Donkey hawking saw-dust to those who butchered beef or cured bacon, the men of Blackpool and the Red City of Gurranabraher walking and whistling their way to work. A bit like living in a musical…but that was a long time ago, a time when people were buttoned up in the days before Velcro.

Somewhere, somehow, something changed with the death of a child, when flesh and bone gave way to rubber and steel, and the people of our street lost sovereignity to the motorcar.

The families were pushed out, out to the reservations in the wastelands. Ironically, where once my friends and neighbours played now stands a multi-story car-park, keeping the car safe from people.

In my mind's eye, Cork is a Josef Keyes painting; looking westward from Bell's Field at sunset. Framed by the salt and pepper cellars that are the belfries of St. Anne's and the North Cathedral, the rolling Northside laid out before me like a table at Christmas time, vanishing over the hill at Knocknaheeney and Blarney Street.

Bolts of pleasure and pain as my memories travel across Brewery Valley from the Bishop's Palace to the dome of City Hall, stopping off along the way at the North Mon, Eason's Hill, Murphy's Stack and land-locked Poulraddy Harbour. Then all the way back to Redemption Road and over the city to the spiked spires of Holy Trinity, Saint Finbarre's and the green tops of Saint Francis.

My city is a Royal town dressed up in crimson. In the distance the County Hall scraping clouds, picking up the gold of a dying sun. And out along the Lee Valley to the Carrigrohane Straight, there, like a last grasp at life, a setting sun sends flames of red and orange and yellow licking high up into the sky. Looks like Ballincollig's burning.

Cork, for me, will forever be the aromatic blending of the Brewery, Linehan's sweet factory, Bracken's bakery. Cork is the sing-song sound of people talking. Cork is the Bells of Shandon and Seamus Murphy's water trough for dogs. Cork is the chimes of an ice-cream van across on Spangle hill. Cork is a skinful of watering holes for when the legs need a rest and the mind needs exercise. Cork is a fine feed of offal. Cork is Noelle Feeney. Cork is Kent Station when a cup or trophy of triumphant victory is coming home, and that's exactly it. Cork is home, there's no place like it."

The writer Conal Creedon lives on Devonshire Street in Cork city centre. He is the creator of the RTE Radio series
"Under the Goldie Fish", author of the acclaimed novel "Passion Play" and many other works.

Dr Chris Luke

"The Accident and Emergency departments of this island are gradually collapsing from the weight of work. It is just relentlessly getting worse and worse. I can compare it to the Titanic syndrome, where the staff are the third-class passengers locked beneath the decks and going down with the ship.

I basically work all over the place but mainly I work in CUH and the Mercy Hospital. Part of the problem is that you've got too few doctors. We have about one-third of the doctors we need, so, all the doctors that work here are doing several different jobs. I work in the Mercy Hospital and I work in CUH, where I am also an educationalist. I had to develop the Accident and Emergency department in the Mercy Hospital from scratch because there was no consultant here when I first arrived four years ago, which means you have to collect stationery, train the nurses...everything.

Today, I have just seen 10 patients quickly. I parachute in, I grab anyone who can walk around the corridor – as opposed to those who are sick or on trolleys – and I quickly process them. Really quickly, but then there is no X-ray person there, so they have to wait another two hours! Why is this? Nationally, we are short-staffed by up to 30%: we are short 5,000 nurses and growing. Nationally, we are massively short of doctors. Why? The universities haven't been funded for medical school training for decades and the only money they really get is from overseas. 60% of our students now are overseas doctors and, of them, 10% to 15% go straight back to their home place. In Cork, 90% of medical students are female – there weren't enough males to field a football team recently! – and of them, up to a quarter will leave medicine within a couple of years. So, we are condemned to a dwindling workforce but at the same time the doctors are screaming for more help. The lack of efficiency is the bottom line: no matter how fast we work – like hamsters – there are not enough of us.

Personally I work 50 to 60 hours per week. But, I'm fundamentally optimistic. Cork is a relative Nirvana compared to Liverpool or Dublin. It is a beacon of peace and tranquillity. We get a steady trickle of violence. Violence on the streets is not that bad and it is containable; it's actually better than it was two or three years ago. We are beginning to see the people who have problems with cocaine, which is becoming a steady trickle. When you take cocaine, you are gone, you are missing, you think you can handle anything. In the book 'Dr Jekyll and Mr Hyde,' the author is taking cocaine: it is the experience of some guy being turned from a gentleman into a monster.

Cork is a wonderful place to be. I spent 10 years in Liverpool, inner-city Dublin, Scotland, where they both had very bad drug problems: there were needle attacks in Dublin; we would have to travel into the flats in Edinburgh in a convoy: a lot of shootings, bodies dumped in people's cars and told to drive to the hospital and just dumped at the door of the hospital…in comparison, Cork is a delightful place to be: it is a lovely city, absolutely booming, bustling in every way. It is really on the up, in the way Dublin was in the late 1980s; the Temple Bar phenomenon. Temple Bar marked the beginning of Dublin's healthier days and Cork is now seeing this with the City of Culture."

Dr Chris Luke is an Accident and Emergency Consultant with the Southern Health Board. Originally from Dublin, he worked for a number of years in the UK before returning to Ireland. He lives in Ballintemple with his wife, Joan, and their four children.

Seán Ahern

"We were selling the houses for £40,000 each, and we could barely flog them. But we needed £200,000, we needed five houses, because then we'd have had the critical mass to go through with the whole thing. And we'd a tough time. But we'd a great builder as well, the late Pat Hennessey. Pat would go away and keep building, and I'd say to him, 'Pat, I've no money to pay you.' And he'd say, 'Yerrah you'll find it from somewhere.' We did always get it somewhere! We're lucky in a way that the people involved in it could work together in partnership and were willing to take risks together. There were many days we didn't have a bob.

A sale blew up at one stage, and we were owing a million to the banks. Back in the days when no one owed a million to the banks. We got the cheque at the very last minute. And that started it all, really.

My father did all sorts of odd jobs. There was no employment, nothing doing in Ireland at that time. He used to be the town clerk, and he used say that the Town Hall couldn't go on fire because it was too damp. They didn't have the price of a typewriter: that was Clonakilty then. You used have houses abandoned on the street because nobody wanted them.

Clon, in particular, got a whacking in the late '70s. The major employer in the town, paying savage wages, so much so that people were thinking of returning from abroad, closed down.

It had been making wallpaper. That knocked the heart out of Clon for 10 years.

Mine was the first generation that was able to stay home and make a bob. That's all forgotten now. People paying taxes at 60% and 70% back in the '70s, interest rates at 18%. There was nothing. They used kill each other that time for an hour's overtime. There were nearly fellas found dumped behind the workplace in the morning.

I would claim that CJ Haughey and Dermot Desmond bred the Celtic Tiger. That's the sort of stuff you needed in this country. The thing was dead. We were the first class ever to emerge from secondary school here in Clonakilty and not have to emigrate. But having said that, the next generation then, in the 70s and 80s, they had to go. I had two brothers and sisters who went to London.

We were lucky; we held on, despite high tax rates and that sort of thing. But we needed Haughey. Even though we'd no money, he put courage there, leadership. It's not the army, it's the man. And he inspired confidence. That's what we wanted, and he mightn't be flavour of the month now, but he did it when it was wanted.

But it's running away now. We've tons of money. We're obese 150 years after the Famine, imagine that! Young people now will never dirty their hands. Picking potatoes? Thinning beet and turnips? Plucking chickens? Plucking chickens was a way of making a few bob for Christmas. Kids did anything for a shilling. Now, there's so much money, just thrown at them. 'An lámh agus an lámh eile' is all the Irish that young people know now."

Businessman Seán Ahern has lived in his native Clonakilty all his life, but for a brief period at boarding school in Wexford. The Faxbridge development, in which he was a partner, was one of the first of the major holiday home schemes that boosted the West Cork economy in the 1990s. He has been involved in property ever since, having worked previously for CIE and Irish Life.

Eileen O'Brien

"We work with men aged between 18 and 40. Most of the guys we work with have some level of dependency or addiction, because that's probably been a contributing factor to getting involved in crime. Some of them have already begun to look at their dependency or their addiction. Some of them have been to prison in the past, have abstained for a while and maybe have relapsed; and the cycle goes round. Many of them are very determined: 'That's the last time I'm going to be locked up and I'm definitely going to get it together.'

I suppose sometimes it's about working with them and challenging belief systems, because as long as they stay in a kind of 'victim place' they will always be 'done to' rather than being in charge and saying, 'I can actually make a different choice.'

We've a very broad, holistic approach to rehabilitation and reintegration back into mainstream life. Because ultimately, their needs are the same as all of ours: money in their pockets; they want to be able to go out with their girlfriends or their partners; they want to be able to set up home; and they just want to be ordinary; and they want to be able to look at you eye-to-eye without shame or despair of what their previous experiences brought them to.

Cork is small and every community in itself is smaller again. If you're from, say, Churchfield, then that's your little patch. At one level, the familiarity is what you need when you come out because that's what you know. One of the positive things about coming back into a small community is that the networks they know often provide the stepping-stones. Like, it's the fella that knows a fella who's looking for a fella to do a bit of work; the generosity sometimes of people to give a chance, to take someone on is unbelievable at times: 'Sure, he's a good person, give him a shot.' That generosity, I think, is still there.

And at another level the familiarity is the greatest threat to slipping back into the life you had before you went into prison. So, it's kind of double-edged, really. Imagine if you were being asked to not talk to the guys that you grew up with all your life, not be around the people that you know and the people that you have, kind of, gained your identification from being with. It takes an awful lot of inner resources to leave all that and to stay at home with maybe just your mother and father watching telly or to develop other interests. It's a really, really difficult thing to do and it can lead to isolation and it can lead to depression and it can lead eventually, without support systems, to fellas going back anyway, because, 'To hell with this: being inside is better. I may as well be still locked up as to be like this.'

Anything that we would do, we'd have to be really respectful around the person. We have to listen attentively to what it is that people are saying, because it's only through listening that we know how we need to respond. And another aspect of it is that we would be very aware of our own cultural bias…I don't know what it's like to stand in their shoes because I haven't been where they've been.

There are days when it's very challenging but it's great fun. They're a great bunch of lads to be around. Any day at the office can be tough but there's an energy around here and it's really, really positive."

Eileen O' Brien works with the Churchfield Youth Community Trust, a post-release service for ex-prisoners.

Pat Falvey

"Let me tell you about Everest. Everest stands at 29,030 feet. The highest mountain in the world. It's at a height at which jetliners cruise. The statistics are very stark: 75% of all people who try her will fail; one in ten will die that get to her summit. And then, people may ask, 'What makes Everest so dangerous?'

What makes Everest so dangerous is avalanches, hundreds of thousands of tonnes of snow and ice that rocks off her face, that can just wipe you out in seconds. Landslides, jetstream winds that come in over a 100 miles an hour, temperatures that go down to minus-60 degrees. Then you have the medical aspects of it: pulmonary edema, where you drown in your own fluids, as some of my friends have done; cerebral edema, where the brain swells up and it actually pushes your brain out through the top of your head and your eyeballs out through their sockets.

But the most dangerous thing you will find on Everest is way more sinister than all that - the same as anywhere in life - your team and yourself. If you're 70 days with someone on the side of a mountain, and you're not compatible, then he'll drive you crazy, and you're definitely going to drive him crazy. So, people say, 'Are you afraid?' and I'd say, 'I'm always scared, but I don't climb mountains to die, I climb mountains to live.'

When I was walking out of Everest in 1991, there was this guy walking in and he was 85 years of age. He was a Welshman, his name was John. We had tea at the Buddhist Monastery at Tengboche on the way to Everest base camp. So later, this woman came across - her name was Jane – and I said to John, 'Who's that?' and he said, 'That's my girlfriend, Pat.' When I asked her what age she was, she turned around and said she was 79 years of age. So, here's an 85 year-old and a 79 year-old who still live to climb to the utmost of their abilities, while at the same time, I have 40 year-old friends who are couch potatoes.

It was one of the most exciting moments of my life, to stand on a patch of ground the size of a snooker table, six miles high in the sky, the height at which jetliners cruise. 65 million years ago, the summit of Everest was on our deepest seabeds and it was pushed with great tectonic force to the sky. So, you could say that I was standing at the bottom of our sea on top of the world. For a small part of time of the history of man, I, as a Norrie, or as a Corkman, stood on top of the world, and there will be no person higher than I was in 1995.

It brought back to me, as I stood and I turned and I pivoted on that pinnacle of ground, what my father professed, and what I profess now: 'To dream and dream big. But remember, that it's in the following of the dreams that success lies.'

I go so I can get away. After a week of winds and minus temperatures, you're going to forget all about mortgages and all the other things, and the one person you're going to be with is yourself, and that's the God within you. And that's what brings me to the coldest, loneliest, most remote places on this planet. That I can be, for a small period in my life, with Pat Falvey. I have found what I was looking for, and that was within me. All these expeditions are part of finding me."

Pat Falvey is best known as a mountain climber. In all, he has undertaken 38 expeditions around the world, "to the coldest, loneliest, most remote" places on the planet. He left school at 15 to become a millionaire, a target he met in his early 20s, before going bankrupt. He rebuilt his business again, retired at the age of 40 and is now a 'professional' adventurer.

Dr John O'Mahony

"Riverdance mirrors the Ireland that we've seen emerge over the past few years, because it's cross-fertilising. This is not purely the thoroughbred 'Irish' dance. The very best of Irishness is evident in it: it's forward-looking, it's outward-looking, it's confident, it's ambitious, and it mixes with great dances of other countries. It's a step on from the crossroads, Kilfenora Céilí band and whatever. This is at a new level, with a great, sophisticated art to it. There is so much authentically Irish about it that you feel proud when you see it.

I was in university in the late '60s and early '70s. It was a very exciting time, it was a radical time. There was new thinking about most things and I was one of the people who was, in many respects, out on the front, out in the fight, on all sorts of crusades, as a student activist – albeit a member of the hallowed Fianna Fáil party!

At that time, of course, politics in student life had an edge. We threw ourselves into it, immersed ourselves into it, took it very seriously. We got hot under the collar and we had great debates, great engagements, if I can put it like that. Sometimes we'd find ourselves in hot water, but that was enjoyable, and I loved it. I was on the Fianna Fáil side, but there were tremendous figures on all sides, stuff like Maoism and whatever. There would have been some very prominent figures on that side of the argument, but I would have enjoyed debating with them and pitching in the traditional line. We did it with a gusto and an edge that made it exciting.

I was born in the heart of West Cork. I attended primary school in Béal na mBláth, eight miles from Bandon. Lovely place, lovely people; God's own people, as they would say. It's the place I love and would go back to every time it's possible. I spend a lot of my time in Dublin, because a lot of my practice is, understandably, in Dublin, but I go back, and I still keep my eye on the local teams: Cloughduv for hurling and Kilmurry for football.

It was solid Fianna Fáil territory. My family had a strong Republican tradition. My grandfather's homeplace would have been the headquarters of the old Republican movement at wartime. Civil war politics have really died at this stage, but nevertheless, the tradition was strong when I was growing up. I personally have retained a very strong Republican and nationalist tradition, and I'm very proud of that.

This country is now blossoming with the finest of the bloom. We are one of the great nations of the earth. Other people who would have said once that we were one of the poor nations are now looking to us for guidance as to models to be adopted by their countries on how they could devise the financial miracle to drive their economies forward.

It is great to be Irish now. Irish people are proud everywhere, in New York, in Shanghai, in Tokyo, in Paris. Anywhere you go, Irishness is a proud badge to wear. It's not only Patrick's Day now, it's every day. We are a country that came from way down the ranks to be one of the foremost nations of the earth."

Dr John O'Mahony, one of only a handful of Irish people with qualifications in both medicine and law, is a Senior Counsel with offices in Dublin and Cork. He first became Dr O'Mahony before returning to college to do law degrees, while practicing as a doctor. While studying law, he was also a member of Cork Corporation, on occasion acting as Deputy Lord Mayor. He and his wife Louise Bennett have two children.

Mary McCarthy

"I've always liked Cork, but I think that there's a difficult side to it as well. Cork is a difficult city to live in. I think Cork is very poetic, it's very beautiful. I like the light here, I like the architecture here. I like walking around town; I bought a house near the city centre.

It's a good life here. But that said, I would have to say that there are challenges in living here. There's incredible smaller-city intensity sometimes. The cynicism of Cork can be quite crippling.

I would consider myself a Cork person, but being from West Cork, you never fully can, can you?! There's certainly a perception that people here are clique-ish and hard to get to know. Certainly there are groups of people. There's an ambiguity about people here; maybe people are less direct here than in other places. They always suss you out. Cork is a place which is quite suspicious of success and people moving on.

But I think there's a lot changing here. It's a hard city to live in, but many other places are too. Cork has suffered such a troubled history in many ways. Its relationships with other places are complex and difficult, its relationship with Dublin in particular. So, very often there's a perceived chip on the shoulder here, particularly with people who don't ever leave Cork to live or work anywhere else. You have to fight that defensiveness alright, that attitude of recklessness that Cork can bring.

Maybe that's just a kind of second-city syndrome. But I think there's a new generation of people in Cork now who are positive, who have never known unemployment, who have never had to go away. Young Cork people are proud to be here: they are articulate, able, not defensive, very mobile. They have a new outlook. I think there's a shift between people who are between 11 and 16 now, and people in my generation.

I was always kind of drawn to art. I used to read a lot when I was younger. Growing up in West Cork, there was always a lot of artists around. So meeting artists was never a separate part of life. I think that's the special thing about the Cork region: there's so many artists living there and contributing to the economy; it's not something you have to make a conscious decision to go out and find. It's always there.

I came back to Dublin in 1993. Dublin was in a boom at that time, and it was a very exciting time to be there, actually. Dublin was a very, very energetic place to be at that time. Temple Bar was coming together, IMMA was three years old. A lot of spaces, a lot of artists, a lot of interest in the arts. So, it was a very exciting time to be around. Very vibrant.

It was a period of growth and in a way you sense a similar energy in Cork now, with things coming together. A sense of possibility. I think it's the coincidence of a number of things. The city is developing, you can see that. When I came back here in 1996, it was a very different place and I think of that quite often. I remember coming into town on Sundays and there was very little open: no cafes, shops, restaurants. That changed in the late '90s, and now, the city centre is booming."

Mary McCarthy, from Whitehall, Church Cross, near Roaringwater Bay in West Cork, is the Deputy Director of the Cork European Capital of Culture Project 2005. She previously worked for commercial galleries in the US before returning to further her studies in Dublin. She then worked in the Irish Museum of Modern Art and was appointed director of the National Sculpture Factory in 1996 before taking up her current position.

Donal Vaughan

"The village is totally in Cork because at the end of the village there is a bridge and once you cross over the bridge you're into Kerry. There's a sign on both sides of the bridge: 'Welcome to Cork,' 'Welcome to Kerry.'

But Ballydesmond parish is divided between the Cork and the Kerry boundaries, which causes fine commotion when it comes to Munster finals and things. Testing times when it comes to the football alright! Great banter. Especially in the bars. It never gets out of hand. It's all in good nature, but nobody gives an inch when it comes to the football. Kerry will give us the hurling alright. But they won't give us the football too easy.

Hannah - my wife - when she came out from Ballyheigue, the first couple of times on the eve of a Munster Final or something, she couldn't get over the rivalry and the atmosphere and the craic: shouting down from one side of the bar to the other; comments flying; plenty of wit. But she thought t'was the best thing ever. She never saw anything like that back in Ballyheigue. You know, when you're not near a border it's not the same.

About 1995, my mother decided that she'd concentrate on the post office because she wouldn't be able to balance the two of them. She asked me would I be interested in doing the shop side of it for a while and I said I'd give it a lash and see how it goes and I'm still here.

I'm Ballydesmond born and bred. I just think I come from a great part of the county. It's special. It's unique: the fact of being on the border of Cork and Kerry but there being a great bond of people here from both sides. There's a great community spirit in the parish.

It's just in the people. I think you don't learn it. It's just in you. I think it's just a natural thing, probably from parents, breeding, handed down from generation to the next generation. It seems to be with us all the time. I mean, the community centre, the housing for the elderly, the housing scheme, the newly-opened crèche, the GAA pitch…I could go on, but all of it involved unbelievable community spirit to get them things up and running. The individuals just had vision and for a small little place with a small population, I think it's great going.

I'd say 'tis just a thing that's bred into you from the olden days. It might be down to the historical side of it from the time of the War of Independence and things like that: going back there was a great fighting spirit here that time. This village was built specially by the English back in eighteen thirty-something. The Black and Tans actually burnt three houses in the village here. They set fire to them the time of the troubles. This house was one of them.

I'd say it's just a natural thing that people look out for each other and they back each other up. The spirit will always be there, I'd say. It'll never go. Listen, it's there, and when it's needed it just jumps out at you. Whether it's a joyful or a sorrowful occasion, it comes to the fore. It does impress all the time; it never fails to impress. I suppose it's hard to describe or hard to put in a nutshell but I just say, 'A great little village, a great parish and a great population.'"

Donal Vaughan is a shopkeeper in Ballydesmond on the border between Cork and Kerry. He and his wife, Hannah, have one son. His mother, Ann, runs the post office in the village.

Denis 'Dino' Cregan

"I hold the record in Greenmount School for not going. It's no boast, but it's a record. I left school when I was 13 and a half and my first job was in UCC, weeding the gardens. So, I went directly from Greenmount School to UCC. And I worked with the great Mick Barry, the bowler. I went into CIE in 1956 as a boy. I was a boy then until I was 20: I was in the Statue Hut for four years. I left CIE in 1967 and I bought my own pick-up truck. I started collecting furniture and delivering stuff and everything for people around the town. And then I opened my first chip shop in 1970.

I was watching Lennox's and I learned from that. I found a house in Tower Street, knocked the garage alongside it and built it with my own two hands, bit by bit. I started in 1969 and I opened on the second of March 1970, my first chipper, Dino's. Why's it called Dino's? The Italian for Denis. But I'm not Italian: I'm anything but.

We didn't know what Government was then. Government wasn't an issue, tax wasn't an issue. If you were starting today, you'd have 16 different organisations in around your arse. I just started. How much did I have the first night I opened? £11 was a great wage at that time: tradesmen were getting £12 a week. How much did I start with, in Dino's in Tower Street? I had £55 that night. I was nearly 30 years old and I didn't know the difference between the chips and the bucket they were inside in.
I bought the fat for the shop above in Daly's of Shandon Street.

And they came in next morning to ask me did I want more fat and I said I was going up to the factory to get more. £30 a box. He said, 'I can give you 10 boxes and I can give 'em to you on credit.' 'What do you mean by credit?' I said. 'You don't have to pay 'til the end of the month'…I'm after making an awful lot of money out of credit. I'm after making an awful lot of money. I'm a very wealthy man. But I don't suffer from any illusions. None at all. I still want to do what I do. I don't want to be anybody else and I don't suffer from any illusions. That's the way I am.

I love public life. Love doing what I'm doing, love every minute of it. Get all the abuse and I take it in my stride. I've been a senator for 20 years and I was in Garret Fitzgerald's book as one of the finest backbenchers he ever knew. And it was all Cork. If it hadn't got anything to do with Cork, I wasn't interested. All Cork: the hell with the rest.

I've been Lord Mayor of Cork, which isn't an honour, it's a privilege. That, to me, was the proudest moment of my life: no doubt about it. Every second when I was Lord Mayor was going too fast, every second of every day.

You have to take local government seriously. I sat at a meeting one night when we were talking about the Lower Road and how we were murdering it with the traffic. And I was sitting across from a fella who put his head back, closed his eyes and said, 'Yerrah, I think we should move the railway station altogether.' And he was an Alderman. That was a great lesson to me: 'Move the railway station altogether.' The biggest engineering feat ever in Ireland, in 1860, was getting the railway line into Cork. Biggest engineering feat ever in Ireland. Sixteen men died to do that, build that tunnel. And an Alderman said that we should move it?"

Denis 'Dino' Cregan is the founder of the famous Dino's chipper chain in Cork and is a Fine Gael member of Cork City Council. There are seven 'Dino's' chippers in Cork city and a drive-through is also planned.

Collette Kelleher

"It can be tough to be homeless in Cork. It's hard to disappear in Cork. For anybody.

Cork is a great size, because it's big enough to be a city, but small enough to be human. You meet people in the shelters sleeping out, and they'll stop you. They'll be upset about something, or they'll have a suggestion to make. Cork's big enough to be interesting and small enough to be intimate. So, you have that kind of immediacy, so you don't have an opportunity to get away from - to be cut off from - the people you're serving.

That's what's better about what I'm doing now, rather than being in Whitehall. Whilst the intention was good, and you had money, there was a removal from the lives of real people, and I found that difficult. You had a government policy, and you had a significant amount of money, and yet, the people you were trying to work it through were kind of disconnected from the people they were serving. I found that difficult.

My hope for Cork in 10 years' time is that it will be a city which is good for everybody, and not just a person who wants to get through the city fast in a car. That has to be accommodated, I'm not in any way a Luddite, but that can't be the only factor.

I was down by South Terrace this morning, there was a woman, in her 80s, trying to get across the road, and these bloody cars, zoom, zoom, zoom. Now, that should be part of the city; that in someone's consciousness, they're thinking: 'What if I'm 80 and I live in the city centre? How do I get around?' 'If I'm homeless, how am I responded to?' 'What if I'm a child?' 'What if I'm a young person?' When I've travelled, I've seen, particularly in France, a great sense of the civic, a thinking-through of a place in terms of the people who need it and use it, rather than as a place where you make money and cars drive through. I'm hoping that, in the Cork of the future, we will have that kind of a city for everybody. That someone, somewhere, is thinking about that 80 year-old woman who lives down on South Terrace and how she gets to the supermarket: does she have to take her life in her hands every time she leaves the front door to cross the road?

I hate getting into national stereotypes, but there's something in Cork, about underplaying things, rather than making them bigger. 'Ah sure, t'will be grand,' even if it's a pretty big thing. 'Ah don't worry about it, we'll get there,' and I think that's helpful, particularly in the work that we do. Instead of saying 'Oh my God, we have to do this, do that,' and getting into a fuss: there is, 'Relax, t'will be alright, girl.' I think that's great. I'm just back from London, and there, living is hard; doing small things is difficult. It is actually physically more difficult: you have to queue longer, there are more people living in a smaller space. But because of that, you get into a mindset of complexity, getting from A to B to C. Yes, because it is actually more complicated, but you begin to think it's more complicated as well. In Cork, you'd say, 'Ah sure that'll be fine. No problem.'"

Collette Kelleher is originally from Macroom. She left in the late 1980s to pursue a career in social work. After undertaking a postgraduate degree in social work, she worked for various community and children's groups, eventually accepting a civil service position as Special Advisor on Early Years in Childhood to the then British Education Minister, Margaret Hodge. She was awarded an OBE by Queen Elizabeth II for her contribution to social work in England. She returned to Ireland to become Director of the Cork Simon Community in 2003.

Martin Fitz Gerald

"In life now, you're only as good as your last match. There's nobody going to come in the door to me because I'm here 160 years or whatever it is. They'll come in if the service is OK. History is a plus sometimes, but if you're not playing well, you won't last.

It was nearly impossible for me to adapt to that. I thought I'd a right one time. It was worst if you grew up in that background, where you're told that you have a right. That's more difficult again. Things change so fast now.

We put a thought for the day up on the door all the time. Now we all realise that there's a point of view out there that's not ours, and that's OK as well. I was one of these fellas who thought that everyone should think the same as me. Got an awful fright when I found out that fellas were doing a lot better when they didn't think like I did. I think that's another good thing that's after opening up now, that if you've a discussion with a person and you disagree, you'll look at it and say, 'we don't agree.' But when I was growing up, if you didn't agree with someone, you wouldn't talk to them. I think that's a great thing now, that people are a bit more outside themselves.

We're here since 1843. We were in Lissarda, and came into Macroom then and have been here ever since, in all different shapes and sizes. From being carpenters, to making nails, to sawmills and timber. They branched out into various things over the years.

When I came along, the hardware business was there, the sawmill, the funeral directing, but it was a different type of funeral directing. There were no funeral homes in those days, it wasn't as professional as what you have now. Basically, you supplied the coffin and the hearse and that was it. It has evolved. The pub was here, but it was tiny: there was no off-licence, no food. We went into the disco business for a while, but got out of it! We keep changing. We'd be very chameleon-like: we follow the money! Well, where we think it is. A lot of the time, it's not there at all, of course.

There was a time when a fella graduated and that was it. 'Where am I going?' they'd say. Now, they're coming back. They're lucky. I've six children and only one of them out of the country. There's a time there were three of them out of the country. And they've all got good jobs. So it's hard to expect people to be as community-based as they were. I suppose everywhere, there isn't the same friendliness, even with the neighbours. Before, you'd walk in and out the door, or the key would be in the door, or there might be no key. If you did that now, you'd have no house.

But at the same time: before, how many farmers were farmers who didn't want to be? How many carpenters were carpenters who didn't want to be? There were professions there as well that people were in but didn't want to be in. I wouldn't think that would happen now: people have the choice. If they want to change, it wouldn't worry me if one of my family came along to me in the morning and said 'I want to sell the section I'm in.' That's up to them. Nothing is there for eternity. You're only as good as your last match."

The Fitz Gerald family name has been synonymous with Macroom for 160 years. Martin Fitz Gerald was only 19 years of age when he took over the family business. He was an only child, and with both parents and grandparents no longer alive, he learned the hard way. Now 60, he has handed parts of the business on to his sons, though he still retains an advisory role.

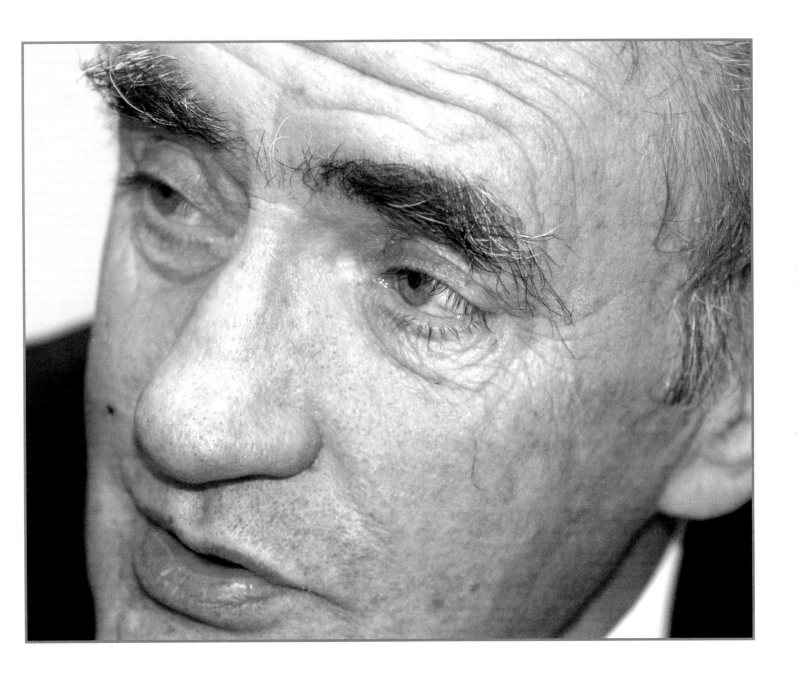

John Spillane

"You're only going to use the most intelligent, the best of the quotes now, aren't you?

I've always liked the Cork writers: Frank O'Connor, his short stories, the translation into Irish, the whole thing about him, Seán O'Faoláin; I love Daniel Corkery, Jimmy Crowley, Jimmy McCarthy, Rory Gallagher. There's enough heroes here: Patrick Galvin, actually, is one of my biggest heroes; I absolutely adore Conal Creedon, I think Conal is just absolutely brilliant; Louis de Paor, my friend. And then there's the Cork Gaelgoirí I hang around with, a small group of people who talk Irish in Cork. There's not a whole lot of them but there's enough inspiration there to do a fella.

That's a good quote! 'There's enough inspiration to do a fella.' There's enough inspiration around here to do a fella for the rest of his life. Every savage loves his native shore, and that's only natural, but I know a lot of people who've left Cork, who didn't like it, who'd give out mad about it, that it's a hole. But I never had that problem. I just love Cork.

It's a constant battle to win over the crowd, and when you get them then, it's fantastic. If there's 100 people there and two of them talking, that's who I want to get. It keeps the thing interesting, because if you go on the run, if you give up, you're just another guy singing in the corner of a pub, and nobody listening to you, which is very demoralising, a soul-destroying feeling.

I would take that approach with people in general, I suppose. A quote of my mother's: 'With patience and perseverance, you could take a donkey from Kinsale to Jerusalem.' I'm in for the long haul. I played in bands when I was a teenager, and in my early 20s, in Cork, and I'm keeping the dream alive, Everybody trails off, gets a day job. But I'm still going for glory, I'm still living the rock 'n' roll dream. I didn't do in my 20s, and I didn't do it in my 30s, but I'm kinda doing it now in my 40s. So, there is a long, slow haul, chipping away at the old block with dogged determination.

I failed English in second year in college. I went to college and did an Arts degree, but I didn't get on well there at all. I got on great with Irish. I loved the Irish department, Sean Ó Tuama was professor up there at the time, the poet, and he was a very inspiring guy, so I learned a lot of Irish. But I didn't like the English degree at all. I didn't realise at the time, but I was in the camp of the enemy. They were teaching me how to be a critic! I wanted to be a creative writer.

I don't really believe in talent, I believe in work. People say to me, 'You're talented,' and I say, 'Not really, like.' I just stuck at it, chipping away at the block. I know some other people in music who I've really, really admired, and I remember going up to one fella and saying, 'It's easy for you, you're brilliant,' but he said, 'It's not easy for me, I just tried and tried and tried.' I'm a believer in the possibility that anyone can do it, well, not anyone, but most people; that it's just a matter of work and determination.

I don't mind doing tough gigs, as long as they're winnable."

Musician John Spillane lives in Passage West, on the 'Cork Riviera' with his wife and daughter. Now in his 40s, this is his third spell as a professional musician. He has released two albums so far, the second of which, 'Will We Be Brilliant Or What', won a Meteor Music Award in 2003. A third album is due to be issued some time in 2005.

Mary Hopkins

"When I was asked to be interviewed for this, I hesitated, to be honest. I've been in the press a lot lately, either for our firm, our client firms, The Rotary Club of Cork, or one of the other organisations I am involved with. I thought this might be over-kill, seen as self-promotion!

Self-promotion is not the preserve of the media classes: it is a modern-day practice in all our lives, whether we like to admit it or not. From our first day at school, right through to old age, we promote ourselves: 'Look at me Mammy'; best foot forward; smile before you dial; slap on the make-up; flashy tie; firm handshake; dress to impress.

I've been involved in the promotion business for almost 25 years now and, to my mind, most people's lives involve some form of self-promotion or other – call it self-preservation, ambition, or a yearning to say your piece or become involved in society. We have a really progressive, self-promoting society now and it is children, oddly enough, who mirror that best. Take Áine O'Driscoll, the ferryman's daughter from Baltimore. She's eight, she's as bright as a button and inquisitive; she epitomises the uninhibited enthusiasm born of the proud pedigree of an islander and a free-spirited upbringing. Adults, on the other hand, can be inhibited, afraid of a 'put down,' and have to make more of an effort to be taken seriously.

There's no room for shrinking violets in today's world; social skills are where it's at. There's no point any more in rearing entrepreneurs and geniuses if they cannot project their talents.

Geoff Read of Ballygowan did it; Maurice Pratt of C & C did it. I worked in a bar with the former and spotted the latter at a disco before my workmate swept him away from my clutches! Even then they were gregarious, outgoing people. Property Developer Owen O'Callaghan does it, the McElhinny Twins do it, and Deirdre Purcell does it – all for different reasons. They aren't egotists: they are pragmatists. They all started with a blank sheet – just an idea – and nobody would know them and their businesses except for their methods of self-promotion through the media, through networking, and through sheer perseverance and hard work.

An elderly gentleman greeted me in Patrick Street one day and suggested that I should cross the street and walk on the sunny side. I did, and it was a sound lesson in life. Let the sun shine in, bask in it, and spread it around. The light makes you look, and feel, goddamn good! Now, that's not to say that I can banish the dark moments in a flash, but it's a help. And you know, walking on the sunny side of the street encourages a cheery slagging en route to work from other city-centre people – Denis at Mac Sweeney's Photo, the lads at O'Flynns' butchers – or a beam from a little nipper in his buggy. Before you know it, life is better, and all because you said the first hello.

Self-promotion can be a means of getting noticed, perhaps if you are starting a new career, are new in town, launching your career or boosting sales in your business, or you're simply having the yen to be heard and taken seriously by a loved one, a peer, or a community. It's better to communicate your 'message' than have it stifled, hindering your progress in life. Let the begrudgers like it or lump it: they're nothing except an excess of hot air.

If I had to sum up? You are your own special person – go walk in the sunlight and watch the reaction."

Mary Hopkins is Chairman of Hopkins Communications, an advertising and public relations firm based in Cork. She is currently President of the Rotary Club in Cork, the first woman to hold the position, and is a member of the board of the Cork Chamber of Commerce. Married to Dave, she has two children, Mark and Judy.

Annette Buckley

"I always wanted to do music, especially songwriting. Coláiste Stiofáin Naofa's music and songwriting course was the only outlet there at the time, 10 years ago. Just basically music and songwriting. I wanted to get involved in that side of things rather than get a degree in it. And then I got my voice trained through the years, with private teachers in Cork, and I've been teaching people myself: that's my bread and butter really.

When I did that course, it really helped me when I started gigging, because they set up gigs for people and put people in bands. Definitely, the scene in Cork is much better than it was. Dublin was always the place you had to play, but I think now Cork is nearly up there, especially with the City of Culture in 2005: that's a really big thing.

I think it's much better now: there're much more venues. For a long time, the Lobby was the only place you could play, or the Triskel Arts Centre. But now there's the Half Moon Club, Cypress Avenue, and there are so many bands coming from abroad and down from Dublin, which gives much more of an outlet for bands that want to get support gigs.

There weren't as many bands before from Cork. There was Frank and Walters, and there was a big push behind them. Then there was a bit of a lull for a while, but I think bands are the main way to go now. You see the Oxegen festival: it's all bands. There's so many bands coming out of Cork now: there's Rulerz of the Planet, Stanley Super 800, Rest, Fred, you could name maybe 20 bands.

Independent labels have changed things. People getting signed isn't such a big thing anymore. Loads of bands now are independently doing it. The Frames and Mundy started that whole craze off, they were at a big label, they got dropped and they ended up doing their own stuff on their own label and doing very well.

Since then, people are piggybacking off that whole thing, and they aren't scared to release stuff any more. There's definitely more of an outlet for it. More artistic freedom, more licence. People are more independent about it, going out and doing it themselves rather than relying on anybody else like a record company to help them out.

There're more promoters coming out of Cork as well. People at the Half Moon Club really want to help new bands out, local bands. There's a record label starting up as well: Blue Monkey. I actually recorded my own album down there, Blue Monkey studios in Ownahinca, which is where Fred recorded their album, Rest as well and so did Rulerz of the Planet. There's loads of bands that have gone down there.

I'm into stuff that isn't mainstream. I think Cork bands at the moment, they're quirky and different. Some of the bands in Dublin, they can be a bit commercial. That's why there was a big push behind them, but now, I think people are latching onto the whole quirkiness thing. That says there's much more out there than just the commercial thing. Now, people are listening to different types of music: underground, lo-fi kind of stuff. Bands that you would never have heard of, and suddenly they're the big thing.

I'll probably never do the mainstream thing ever. I don't think I want to. I do my own thing really. I'm kind of, if you like, a bit of a loner. To say the least!"

Folk singer Annette Buckley hails from the Old Head of Kinsale. She moved to Cork in the mid-90s to pursue a career in music. Her EP, Untitled, was released in 2002, and her debut album, produced independently, with the help of her sister, is due for release in late 2004 or early 2005. In addition, the 29 year-old collaborated with local band Rest on their debut album, 'Burning in Water, Drowning in Flame.'

Anthony Dinan

"We're one of the few remaining major family owned businesses in Cork. Others would include Johnson and Perrott, Barry's Tea and Musgraves.

Only a third of second generation family businesses survive and only ten percent get to the third generation. We are now in the fifth generation. And we got there by being able and prepared to change, being prepared to take what action is necessary and being prepared to invest in the company. That's the only way it could happen.

They say that the first generation makes it, the second generation takes it and the third generation breaks it. That's true unless you have a structure set up where you control the number of people who are going to inherit the shares. Otherwise you can be dealing with each generation, with more and more shareholders, all with different requirements. The Crosbies have kept it very tight in this Company and they are very proud of it. They're very proud of the Cork tradition as well. While we have acquired many papers throughout the country and one in England, we never moved our headquarters from Cork. We are very committed to that.

There were difficult times. We had cutbacks in '84 and '87 and again in the nineties. In fairness to all the staff it wasn't just management who sorted things on its own. People on both sides were determined to find a solution to our problems. That loyalty works two ways. It's a family business and people are helped when they have difficulties as well. You know people better than you would if you were working for a multi-national.

In all that time one of the great things about the shareholders was that even though there were losses accumulated up until 1991, they still reinvested in the organisation during that time. They borrowed money to back the business because they believed the business would succeed. There is huge credit due to them for doing that. Why would people bother doing that unless they were committed to a family business?

Until 1995 we had the Examiner, Evening Echo and Waterford News & Star. Then we started to acquire more newspapers. We acquired the Western People and the next year we acquired the Sligo Weekender. Then we bought in Carlow; Kildare, Laois, Newry and Down. Then came the Sunday Business Post; the Kingdom; Irish Post and the Roscommon Herald. We now have 14 newspapers and a new media division that operates a range of businesses including our websites, a breaking news service, Recruit Ireland.ie and Motornet.ie.

TCH moved into this building, 97 South Mall, four years ago creating a Head Office, and a group structure so that HR, marketing, finance, purchasing and national sales support could be given to all the newspapers - to get synergies by acting as a Group.

The phrase acquire or be acquired is very true. Whether we like it or not the newspaper industry here is condensing down into 8 players. It possibly will condense further into 5 players. If we can't compete with people coming in and buying newspapers then we're wasting our time. We must show that we are a serious player. The vehicle to do that is not any one title but an organisation which feeds services to all titles. That's the way to do it. There are still more newspapers to be acquired. There are about 17 stand-alone titles at the moment. We want to be one of the five players that are left."

Anthony Dinan holds an MSc in Management from Trinity College Dublin. He joined the Cork Examiner in 1980 as Management Accountant and was appointed to the Board of Directors in 1985. He has been Managing Director of Thomas Crosbie Holdings since 1992.

Eddie English

"I feel I'm in the heart of it all, because the sport of sailing began outside the door there in 1720, on literally the water two hundred metres away from us, when they founded the Cork Water Club in Haulbowline Island. I feel very much a part of that tradition.

My memories of my summers are out there: rowing, swimming, fishing, sailing. My first boat was a rowing boat with a sail on it, when I was about 10 or 11, and I graduated to a proper boat then when I was about 12.

I was lucky enough to get into UCC, where I did Commerce. I wasn't sure what I wanted to do. My father and mother were involved in the clothing industry in the city and I knew I didn't really want to do that; underneath it all, I wanted to run a sailing school, but couldn't see how it was economically feasible. In fact, I'm still realising it's not terribly economically feasible after a long, long time as a sailing instructor! I could have earned more money if I was working in the shut-down plant maintenance or the 'Steel, but I was doing what I liked doing and getting paid for it.

I really started sailing in 1973 with the late Denis Doyle, who was one of the famous sailors in Ireland at the time. We went over to Cowes - the Mecca of yachting – and I really got the bug at that stage. The next huge bit of responsibility came to me out of the blue, when Denis said, 'Right, you are taking the boat home,' and I was skippering a 50-foot yacht – one of the biggest racing yachts in the country – on delivery trips back and forth to Ireland. So, I forced myself to learn a lot more navigation and I really grew up in terms of sailing very, very quickly then. My only problem was that my attention to my studies wasn't brilliant and I've a fair history of spending a very long time doing a Commerce degree in UCC, having to repeat in most autumns!

I would have liked to have seen Cobh move forward more, especially with regard to marine tourism: the facilities in Cobh were better 120 years ago than they are now unfortunately. Even when I was in school in the '60s, we had two cinemas in Cobh, we had a theatre, we had a swimming pool in the '70s, and now, we are here in the new millennium, we have no cinema, no theatre, no youth club. The town is marching forward but it lacks these basic facilities. There have been promises, promises, promises, but what's going to happen? I wonder what's the future. I've begun to run courses in Crosshaven and various other places in Ireland – primarily in Crosshaven and Baltimore – and will continue to use venues that have facilities. We badly need a marina, we badly need proper facilities: I think the local authorities really need to pull their socks up.

When I went abroad I thought that was amazing but the great thing was to come home and see that Cobh was as good as anywhere else. To look at, Cobh was as stunning, or more stunning, than most places I visited in England, France, Spain. Abroad, the social side of it is a bit quiet, especially for a person in their 20s: they are a bit sleepy, touristy and didn't have enough vibrancy. But because of the fact there is a homegrown population of 10,000 here, there is always a bit of action in Cobh. It's just a terrible pity that we can't invite boats to come here because we have no facilities for them."

A Commerce graduate of University College Cork, Eddie English runs a number of maritime courses around Ireland. His sailing school is based on the seafront in Cobh, County Cork. He has been heavily involved in tourism in the town for over 20 years.

Freda Hayes

"People often ask me, 'How did you end up as Chief Executive and Secretary of Blarney Woollen Mills?' and I say, 'Just by process of elimination.' My three older brothers at the time were all gainfully employed. I was in school. And basically my father just said, 'I want to start this business but I can't afford to give up my job, so I want you to leave school and come and start this business.'

My father built a shop on wheels and he rolled it down in front of the castle. We were promptly moved, as the owners of the castle weren't too pleased with our audacity to park in front of their gate. And eventually we parked outside here. It wasn't exactly an overnight success: it went on for many years with us nearly going to the wall every six months; starting a business with no equity was a leap of faith.

But that went on for about 10 years and we eventually were sort of getting on our feet and then the mill came up for sale.
We couldn't get the loans to buy it because in that time tourism retailing was unheard of. There were a few small knick-knack shops around the country selling leprechauns made in Japan, but that was it. So the bank thought, 'Not at all. That won't work at all. Mad.' I remember coming out of that meeting with my father, and I saying, 'Jesus, what are we going to do now? I gave a commitment yesterday that we were going to buy it.
I've signed the contract.'

So he scurried around for a month or two and the family just raised the £75,000 ourselves by taking out extra mortgages on our houses or whatever. But I would say within a year or two we knew it was going to work. Immediately the coaches started to pull in. The visitors loved it and we just developed it from there.

Around the same time, my father used to say, 'The worst thing there now is that all the men are mad to get their wives out of the shop because they're spending too much money. We need a pub.' To get a pub licence at that time you needed to have ten bedrooms. So we developed ten bedrooms, we got our pub licence and the guys were very happy reading the paper and having their pint of Guinness while their wives did a bit of shopping.

A lot of people are afraid to take chances. And a lot of people are afraid to fail. I'm not. I was so near to failure so many times.
No matter how smart you think you are, you still fail at some things that you do. So who cares if you fail sometimes? You pick yourself up and get on. My father, Christy, had tried many businesses before this worked. I mean, all his life he had all sorts of vegetable rounds, cinemas, dance halls, hackneys, and as kids we grew up with that. So he had his job but he had all of these other things as well. None of them made any great money.
But they were all a learning exercise. Most people in the village thought he was mad, but eventually, he hit on something.
And when he built the thatched cottage and rolled it down in front of the castle, a lot of people still thought he was mad.
But, you know, I think he never, ever cared about what people thought. He always said, 'Ah I think it's a good idea. We should try it.' He was a great visionary."

Freda Hayes is Chief Executive of Blarney Woollen Mills. She left the company after her father's death in the early '90s, set up Meadows and Byrne and was involved in several other tourism-related business ventures, before returning to the family company in 2000.

Michael Hanley

"I entered into business in the town about 30 years ago. I came into a town that was seriously affected by unemployment. Mind you, it always had a good agricultural hinterland here, but the whole approach to employment and the progress of the town from an economic point of view was absolutely sterile.

So, I set about getting involved in the business life of the community. First of all we resurrected what was the Fermoy Traders' Association. And we did an awful lot of good things from a PR point of view.

In the middle of the '70s, not long after I had come into business, there was a major oil price hike which caused disastrous consequences in inflation. Interest rates shot up to 22% and that had an enormous effect on this town in particular. It made me more determined than ever to tackle the situation. In 1985, I decided to go for election to the local urban council. I was elected on the second count first time out.

I decided, based on my experience working with various groups, that the only way we could tackle Fermoy's problems from an economic point of view was to establish an Enterprise Board. I hand-picked – without any apologies – those people who would have been the main players in any town, in the economic life of the town. We met outside in the empty Beehive factory, as it was at the time, and we decided on a modus operandi. This place was the headquarters. The place is alive with files: years of work, excellent work. You'd be very proud when you look back through it.

The work was confidential. Otherwise, we couldn't have made the progress we needed to make. I found that to be one of the problems, with elected representatives in particular: they're totally shallow. It's easy to waffle, it's more difficult to deliver. I was only keen on delivering. And we did deliver.

One of my key things is to persuade individuals who have done well to put something back into the community. We were fortunate that we had two guys in particular: John McCarthy and Tom Cavanagh. Our first shot was that the IDA brought a major site visit to us from SCI, a company from Alabama. And we had to keep yer man, Olan King, the bossman, a billionaire, and we had to give him solid guarantees on a whole series of issues before he would agree to come here. We duly did that, delivered on it and he promised 450 jobs, but in practice, the number of jobs there has never been below seven or eight hundred.

Fermoy has always had a social deficit, in that we don't have sufficient numbers of professional people living here. So, we're actually targeting that now; we want to get more high-quality jobs in. As you know, the world is changing, and low-grade jobs are disappearing to China and what have you. We don't want to get caught in that scenario.

As a direct result of our competence and success in being able to handle large-scale industrial development, the IDA agreed to buy the old Army Barracks in the town, and they've now spent quite a bit of money on the site for Fermoy Business and Technology Park. We've one idea in particular for that.

I don't like reading about myself. I have a whole team of people who've helped me achieve what we've done. Persuading those who have done well, to put something back was the key all the time."

Michael Hanley was a farmer before buying a newsagent's shop in Fermoy in the 1970s. After his election to the Town Council, he established the Fermoy Enterprise Board to help the town deal with its economic difficulties. Their work with the IDA attracted American firms SCI and MetLife, and French company FCI, to the town. Medical insurance company BUPA Ireland now operates out of the premises which previously housed MetLife. Michael recently topped the poll to return to Fermoy Town Council.

Mary Crilly

"March 8th 1983 was the day we launched the centre. I think what we looked at back then was helping women who had been raped and who were going through a crisis, who might need to go to the guards, who might need to go to court, who wanted crisis help and crisis support.

I hadn't been involved in anything at all like this before. A neighbour of mine, who had been involved and who knew about it, asked me. That's how I came across it. I hadn't even been in a women's group back then. I was living at home on my own with my two daughters, who were quite young.

I think if you'd asked me to put a bet on then, I would have said that I'd last six months, because I really felt out of my depth; I didn't know where I was coming from, or what was needed, what people needed. I remember the very first flag day we had, getting a fair bit of flak on the streets of Cork. People would be saying, 'Do you want to get raped?' or 'What do you want?' or 'What are you doing this for?' Looking back, I don't think people were being abusive, I think they were just very confused, because there wasn't a Rape Crisis Centre in Cork then, and as far as people were concerned, abuse didn't happen, because it was so hidden.

There was a lot of misunderstanding over what we were doing: were we trying to break up marriages? Were we trying to stir up trouble? Whereas now, I think people see that what we're trying to do is, help people to move on with their lives and get back with partners, or being the way they want to be with partners, something they couldn't do before because of what had happened to them.

Nobody comes in and says, 'I want A, B, C, or D.' They say, 'I want to get my life back.' A young woman might come in who says, 'I'm going out with this guy and I'm mad about him, but I can't bear to touch him. I was raped two years ago, but it was nothing to do with him and I feel really bad.' Or he might come in and say, 'I'm going demented, I don't know what to do here.' So, we work with both of them, just support him and help her to get through it. I think if people ask for so little and you're there, able to give, you've a duty to give it to the best of your ability.

I love to see people getting what they need. They leave here, and the abuse is still there, but it's not eating them any more. It's not in their soul, in their heart. Inside, where it's been with them all their life, it's there no longer. And they can move on. They'll never feel as badly as they did before they began counselling.

Speaking now, the people in Cork turned out to be our best ally over the years. We wouldn't have this building only for them. A lot of the money came in pounds and fivers and tenners. There was a lot of real goodwill there: go for it, just go for it and we'll support you every way we can. In 2003, I was awarded the Lord Mayor's Award, by Councillor John Kelleher, who was the Lord Mayor at the time and that was huge, because we were being recognised by the city; and the city was recognising that abuse had happened."

Mary Crilly is the Director of the Sexual Violence Centre, formerly the Rape Crisis Centre. The centre moved to its current location, on Camden Quay in the city centre, in 1997.

Dave O'Connor

" I'm 21 years in the fashion business this year, and I'd say – from day one up to now – every day I go to work - from my days in Coláiste Chríost Rí and with the 'Barrs playing football and hurling – I feel like I'm training for a County final. I put the effort in every day.

I met a fella out in Ballyphehane one day. I was just walking along. Jackie Moore was his name, and he had this type of jacket on which there was a lot of demand for, but no place to buy them in Cork. So, on the inside of the jacket, there was a phone number, and the name of a company. At the time, my Dad was made redundant from his job, and he got something like £9,000. So, he lent me the money and I went over and invested in leather jackets, 20 years ago.

I then went away and I bought a Hiace van, and lucky enough, I got the finance through Dinny Allen, the former Cork player, who believed in me and trusted in me – because he knew my uncle from Nemo Rangers, John O'Connor! It all began when we went over to England with the phone number and the name.

When my Dad was living in London, he was friendly with a priest in Hammersmith. As a result of that, we were left park our van in the church yard. Next door was London Metropolitan Police, and they used have cameras on the yard, so we were totally secured.

There were some fantastic priests in Hammersmith that time; they used work in the Underground with all the down and outs, people who came over to England looking for a crock of gold.

Fr Kiely was a fantastic man; he'd spend his days down in the Underground trying to bring fellas up and get them on the straight and narrow.

What we used do in Hammersmith was that my Dad would drive over to England and I used fly over and meet him over there. Then, Fr Kiely would pick up some youngfella from the Underground that was going through a bad time or wanted to go home – I'd fly him home on my airline ticket, and I'd go home with my Dad. And then, every Christmas in Hammersmith, we used organise a bazaar, and we got all spots from the manufacturers, and all the money used go to the people who were living rough in London and finding it hard to survive. That was our way of saying, 'Thanks.'

We took off from there anyway. The word spread through Cork that we had jackets a third the price of the shop, that they were fantastic quality. So, I converted my shed at home in Togher into a kind of a store, and we traded from there and the van as well.

Then, my brother, Bryan, joined us, and he got this notion that we should move downtown from Shandon Street. But, I felt myself that we weren't right for downtown, that we hadn't got the ability. But then, when I got inside there, I saw how easy it was, compared to where we were because before you hadn't a third of the flow of people.

We always learned one thing as we were growing up: hard work and effort. If you're going to do something, do it right, and put in the effort. From day one, when I started off in my first job – which was with Pat Dawson as an Echo boy – to now, I still put in 100% effort."

Togher-born Dave O'Connor worked as a clothing salesman for Alan Best shortly after leaving school. He was made redundant from that job, but a chance meeting inspired him to set up his own clothes business. His Diesel chain moved from the O'Connor household's back garden to Barrack Street to Shandon Street to "downtown" and now operates eight stores in Cork city centre.

Val O'Connor

"After school I came back to work here and then my father and uncle decided to send me to America, New York. I was at college there for two years and it was really the kind of thing that changed my whole life. This was in the mid-50s and Ireland was very behind the times and quiet.

First of all I was intimidated by the Americans, the way they walked tall and all that, but I found that the secondary education in the Mon was more than equal to the task. After a while t'was my chest that was coming out!

So, I spent two years there and afterwards I worked with a funeral firm there that did 10,000 funerals a year. That would be roughly a third of the whole business in Ireland: that would give you some idea of the scale.

I came back then and I found that the whole experience gave me a different approach to life. I was more positive, more outgoing; t'was, in those days, really a big thing to go to college in the States for a few years, and I have to thank my father and uncle for that.

Then, it came to the stage where my father passed away and I started the first ever funeral home in Ireland in 1967. What happened then was that I took the American style, but adapted it to the Irish model: what Irish people would accept and what they wanted; what was required.

After a few years, we found that our competitors didn't know how to cope with it really, and we took over three firms and absorbed them here. I also started a school for young trainee funeral directors to try to bring them along, because I knew the older people wouldn't be so keen! We now have a presence in virtually every county in Ireland, in the sense that we've trained someone who now works there.

Then, I suppose we really went on from there. Due to the fact that we bought out some businesses, we became involved in property as well and established a property company as a result. We built houses in places like Little Island and Deerpark. We've one development we're working on now outside Castletownroche and we're taking a new, positive look at it. We are putting in solar panels, timber frame and water harvesting. The rainwater will be directed down into the tank underneath and be cleansed: that will take care of 60% of the water needs of a house - all the bits and pieces, except for drinking water obviously. It would be the first big scheme of its kind. I love innovating and doing something new and different; I get a great kick out of that.

I love the Cork humour as well. Dublin has its humour also, of course, but I think the accent has something to do with it; if I tell a Dublin joke with a Cork accent it doesn't work... I suppose I'm not great at telling jokes anyway: I'm better at listening to them!

I'm a very proud Corkman: Niall Toibín made the point one time about Corkmen that they're homesick even at home. I wouldn't be quite that, but I'd often travel to Dublin and to come home, and see the view of the city, the Cathedral, the Holy Trinity and all that: we've a magical city, really. I come to work down Cathedral Road every morning – I live up in Sunday's Well – and to look down onto the harbour and the North and South Channels is wonderful: we have a really beautiful city."

Educated in the North Mon, Val O'Connor is a third-generation funeral director. O'Connor Funeral Homes is situated at the North Gate Bridge, at the bottom of Shandon Street in Cork city centre.

Tim McCarthy

"Feis Maitiú is a music and drama festival, founded in 1927 by the Capuchin Order. The original aim of the Feis was to do with temperance within the tradition of Fr Mathew; needless to say we have moved away from that slightly. We are coming up to our 79th year now. Our aim primarily is to encourage participation in music and drama, that is, in instrumental music, in singing, in speech and drama, both in Irish and English. We are considered to be one of the largest in the country: we have approximately 4,000 performances every year and that would translate to between 15,000 and 17,000 people coming to take part. Our catchment areas are Cork city and county, but we have a number of performers coming from Kerry, Waterford, Tipperary, Galway and Dublin. The majority of participants would be under-18 but we have quite a large adult section as well.

The essential part is that they come to participate. They perform what they have prepared, there is an adjudicator who comes and sits and listens to them, gives them an assessment on their performance and the whole hope is that they will go away and have learned from the performance and obviously improve their standards of performance. It's not just to encourage performance: it's also to encourage the development of the person, because we would hope that their performance in the Feis will help to encourage their sensitivity, their awareness and their appreciation of the arts, mainly music and drama.

A lot of people around the city and the county seem to be connected in some way to the Feis. Yesterday, I was in the bank lodging some cheques and the cashier said, 'It's not that time of year again?' That sort of thing keeps happening. Last January, I was listening to Sunday Miscellany on RTÉ One. This woman had written a story about Feis Maitiú and in her story she was telling about when she was at school: all the build-up and preparation they did to take part in the Feis. She went on to describe the day and then talked about how she's now a mother and she's coming along to the Feis with her children. I thought that was a reflection of the continuation; that it was always there. People know it's there, they understand it, and they would be disappointed if it wasn't there.

It's a long, long history; there's a lot of history there. It's not a big earth-shattering or earth-moving thing, but it is still significant and important in people's lives.

I was in Killarney a couple of weeks ago and the waitress recognised me. It took us a few moments to figure out how she knew me, until she told me she had taken part in the Feis. She had just finished her Leaving Cert and she was going off to London to study Musical Theatre: that came out of her involvement in the Feis. She was from Mitchelstown and she was telling me how every year the Feis was central to her training and because of her exposure, she will go on to study.

And a couple of years ago, I had a phone call from a man who was just back from Australia. He had been in an antiques shop in Adelaide and he came across a Feis Maitiú gold medal from 1929. I thought that was a very significant point, because somebody had travelled to the other side of the world, and had taken the medal with them. It must have meant something special to them."

Tim McCarthy, from Victoria Road, is the administrator of Feis Maitiú, Europe's highest-participation cultural festival. He studied Speech and Drama at the Cork School of Music and holds a BA and H Dip from University College Cork. He is an internationally recognised teacher and adjudicator, having adjudicated at festivals in Ireland, the UK, the Isle of Man, Jersey, Hong Kong, Sri Lanka and Zimbabwe.

Kathleen Lynch

"Years ago I heard a saying that we all eventually end up half a mile from where we started off. Whether that's because people come back to be buried, or whether they come back to where they originally belong, I don't know, but in my case it's true, because I can now see where I was born and reared from my window. In Cork, it's truer than anywhere else; I think the city is so small that we all do eventually end up half a mile from where we started off.

I grew up in what was called Spangle Hill until they had a plebiscite to change the name to Farranree. There were difficulties in relation to how others saw us, maybe because of people who ended up in court for shoplifting, fighting, drunk and disorderly – the stuff which gets a mention in the bottom line of any court report. People that were promoting the name change in the area thought it was a difficulty of perception: 'If we change the name, then the poverty will go away and the behaviour that comes with poverty will vanish.' Of course, it didn't.

I suppose what made me become involved in politics was the rampant poverty that was there. I was the youngest of 11 and a lot of them were married before I came along, so therefore the poverty didn't effect me at that level at all, but going to school in Blackpool, the poverty was…it was no shoes. And, this was the early '60s now.

It was like Frank McCourt's book, 'Angela Ashes,' which I didn't like, I must admit. But the one thing that the book did, it crystallised something very clearly for me: that children as well as adults can be deeply offended, deeply offended by the attitudes of adults, and they feel indignation every bit as deeply as adults do. I can still see a particular family of children, one brother and two sisters – now there was a lot more of them in that family, but these were the three that went to school with me. Everything about their world was infused by poverty. Everything.

When the rest of us went home for lunch at one o'clock, they sat in the schoolyard – sometimes in the biting cold – and they had a slice of bread. That's what this awful, awful grinding poverty is all about. Then, when I saw these people coming along and asking to change the name of the area because somehow they thought that by changing the name, you would rid of the problems that are endemic and caused by poverty? It made me laugh really. But that's where I got my interest in politics.

Not everyone survived it. Others didn't succumb to it – they didn't die as a result of it – but a lot of people didn't come out dancing for joy either. While we were canvassing in recent years, I knocked on a door, quite a bit away from here – not within the half-mile – and this woman answered the door and I knew her. I said to her, 'Oh, is this where you are now?' And she pretended she didn't know me. I knew this person; I grew up with this woman. She pretended she didn't know me and I said, 'I must've had the wrong person,' and I walked away. The problem was that she hadn't travelled far enough from the poverty to be comfortable with where she came from. So, not everyone survived it. And not even the second generation totally survived it."

Kathleen Lynch, from Spangle Hill – now Farranree – the "spoiled youngest" of a family of 11, is a Labour Party TD for Cork North-Central. She lives in Blackpool, and has three daughters, a son and two grandsons.

John A Murphy

"I never knew anyone who left saying they were dissatisfied with living in Cork. People would see no reason why they should leave Cork because, as far as they're concerned, it is self-sufficient.

You won't find people ever comparing Cork to Dublin very much because there's no need to, really. Even the use of the phrase 'Southern Capital.' People say there's no such thing, but its frequent use indicates that people find that a very satisfying thing.

There's no doubt, in my view, that it's the city that gives the personality to the county, not vice versa. The city is at the centre in more than a geographical sense. And city people, to make another generalisation, are more self-assured, more confident, more cocky, than their county cousins: the county are only poor relations. Niall Toibín's description of them, probably not meant in any disparaging way, was, 'Kerrymen with shoes.' For people from the city, civilisation crumbles at Carrigrohane, Macroom is ultima thule and dragons lurk at Mushera.

The country people see city people as kind of urban smart-alecks, cute – in the Irish sense – cunning, devious, wily, garrulous, opinionated, smug. There's a famous story about the taxi driver who takes this American tourist on a ride around the city and drops him back to the hotel, and the American pays him a big fare, looks at his money and ruefully says, 'I never knew Cork was that big.' Taxi driver says, 'Big, sir? No one knows the size of Cork…'

Perception and self-perception is hugely important: if Cork people feel that they have certain personality characteristics, they tend to act up to those, play out the part.

Outsiders' perceptions of all that aren't always very favourable. In, 'The Tenets of Time,' by the late Irish-American, Tom Flanagan, which is largely set in the Macroom area, one of the characters is made to refer to the city as a 'vainglorious Lilliput,' a phrase which stuck in my mind, with all the implications of self-deception of the people who think they're great.

Those who have experience of Cork's sometimes vicious and petty intellectual circles would not be very positive in their descriptions of what these characteristics are. Seán O'Faoláin, who had some experience of what we might describe as intellectual life in Cork, said that to survive in Cork you needed 'the agility of a hawk, the speed of a hare, the skin of a rhinoceros and the dissimilation of a crocodile.'

In a way, the Cork thing transcends class. The accent, even, transcends class and education. Obviously there are minor gradations: the tone of the accent ranges from the rich plumminess to the asthmatic whine, but, nonetheless, it's the one accent, and a source of great pride. There's no mistaking the utter distinctness of a Cork accent. And the failure of outsiders to imitate it properly – they make desperate attempts – is a source of pride. The BBC, in their marathon series on the English language, had this thing about factory workers in Blackpool in Murphy's Brewery and the people in Blackpool, on balance, were more delighted that they needed subtitles than resentful that they couldn't be readily understood.

There's lots of old stories which are used to illustrate all that self-confidence. The one I like is about the father telling his son, when he's leaving Cork to go to Dublin for a job, 'In company, don't be too inquisitive. Above all, never ask people where they're from. If they're from Cork, they'll tell you, if not, you don't want to embarrass them.' There's a lot of truth in that."

John A Murphy is Professor Emeritus of Irish History in University College Cork. Born and raised in Macroom,
he has lived in the city for all of his adult life.

Gerry Kelly

"In 1978, I came from one of the richest countries in Europe to one of the poorest. At that time, when I arrived here, Dunlop's closed, Ford's closed: it was a dark period economically. But strangely enough, at that time, Bridget Doolan was Director of the Cork School of Music, and things were on the up there and did improve there steadily through the '80s: despite the various cutbacks, there was a sense of feeling and appreciation from the people of Cork and also there was a sense that we were really doing something.

So, it was such an anomaly for me to then hit a crisis in the School of Music a few years ago when the economy was booming: we were offered a building and then, all of a sudden, our dream goes up in smoke.

We were moved from the old building across to Union Quay. The Hardiman Group had done a huge review of what was going on in the school to see was a new building justifiable, or should it be an extension, or whatever. So, eventually, there was to be this huge new building on the site of the School of Music for Cork 2005. Then, we hit this huge crisis. And I moved from being this persona of a cello teacher and cello player to what I call being a cultural activist.

I suddenly found myself leading this campaign, which got enormous public support. Everybody in Cork must have made a phone call, written a letter, stopped a politician in the street or done something; there was a tremendous showing of support. There was huge support from the media. I still have a lot of the press clippings: there were literally acres.

The school has been in existence for 125 years. So, we've literally touched every single family in Cork, directly or indirectly. Either a member of them has gone to the School of Music, or they have been taught by a graduate of the School of Music, or we've played at a birth, wedding, public occasion, whatever. It showed us that music in Cork is very dear to the people, because, otherwise, they wouldn't have got involved. And what it means in terms of the new building is that it clearly belongs to the people. This idea of it belonging to an elite group of classical people is forever broken. It quite clearly belongs to the people: they took the action and they got it.

I'd like to dispel for once and for all a rumour going around Cork for the last 25 years that I dress up as a gorilla. The gorilla is known to probably fifty or sixty thousand children. The children know it's not me and, I would think that only a woman would get into a gorilla suit and play the cello, that's really all I can say about that. For the schools' concerts, the gorilla is always part of the concert, because there's a perception about classical music and concerts in City Hall. If you tell a child, 'You're going to go now to a classical concert in City Hall,' you'll get, 'I don't wanna go, I wanna go to McDonald's.' But if you tell the child that the gorilla is playing in City Hall, they'll all want to come and see it. Now, the amazing thing about the gorilla is that she never plays badly - always behaves badly, but can play the most serious classical music and get the undivided attention of the children. It kind of shows that if you want to reach a child, you have to do it through imagination."

The cellist Gerry Kelly is a teacher in the Cork School of Music since 1978, when he returned to Ireland from West Germany.

He is married to the broadcaster and musician, Evelyn Grant. All four of their children work in music.

Maurice Healy

"In 1993, interest rates went through the roof. The summer of '93 will go down in business terms as the worst one of my life. We had stock coming in from Japan and interest rates at one stage went up 100% overnight. We'd borrowed to do the acquisitions, we'd stock coming in, people froze when the rates went up, the stock kept coming in, so we wound up with a warehouse full of stock and no cash. So, we had to re-jig and concentrated very much on the services side of it during that summer, just to stay alive.

Eventually we stopped the orders, but it took us right through that year to get rid of the stock. By Christmas, we were back OK again, but the summer of '93 was sitting on the edge of the bed at night holding your stomach wondering how you're going to be in business the next day. But we got through it. Once you survived that period, when the uplift came in '94 and '95, you were well-placed. And then the world just went mad.

When we floated first, it was grand: we were moving nicely. Then the dotcom boom came, and we suddenly became sexy all of a sudden. It's really hard to believe: at that time, we were actually trying to dampen people's expectations. Normally you're trying to build it up and rally, but we actually found ourselves in the situation of trying to calm everything down. Crazy time.

The share price was something like £5 and within six months it had gone from £5 to £15 and went up to £18. So I sold a load of shares when it was at £18 and they asked, 'Why?' And I said, 'We're good, but we're not that good. You can't treble the value of the business in six months: it doesn't make any sense!' So I sold out, thinking it would come back down and I could buy back. It went to £25 sterling after that. The most lunatic time you'll ever come across.

Then the squeeze came on. We were operating at that stage all over Europe. I was flying all over the place and had sold a lot of shares, so I was no longer the big shareholder by that stage. So, in 2001, I decided to buy back the Irish operation again and rebrand it as Calyxx. We turnover €60-odd million in Ireland and employ about 200 hundred people.

I was spending so much time going around Europe that I was in the classic syndrome of waking up in the morning wondering 'Jaysus, what city am I in today, who am I here to see, what am I doing?' And I was in airplanes for three days a week. And I didn't own it any more. I was still a shareholder, but a very small shareholder, so I was more like an employee and I wasn't getting the same buzz out of it. I bought it back myself so it's my own business now.

When I was in Coláiste Chríost Rí there was a guy who had Dawson's Shop down at the end of Friars' Walk. We used to deliver papers for him. So after school, we went door-to-door with the Evening Echo to Joe Murphy Road and Nuns' Walk and all those areas, just shoving them through letter boxes. And you did it every night and collected the money on Friday. I got twelve old pennies for doing it the first time. It crept up after that, but not too much!"

Maurice Healy, from Cork city lives with his wife and two children in Dublin. His company, Calyxx, has offices in Dublin, Cork and Limerick. At one stage a bookmaker, he decided to take a degree in Computer Science in Trinity College, Dublin, in the late '80s. He founded a technology company, ITG, after graduating. His parents, Joan and Michael, still live "out the Lough."

Dr Clare O'Leary

"It's just huge excitement and exhilaration and emotion: when you're on the trek in, you pass these huge mountains and suddenly you're up there and you're looking down on all of these and they're just sort of peaking through the clouds and it's absolutely incredible.

I suppose we were there for about 20 minutes altogether. I couldn't see enough; I was just looking around. And to just sit there and enjoy it, it's amazing. And to see the Sherpas: we think that they're really strong and they've no problems with altitude, almost assume that they're going to make it. But Everest is almost something religious to them. And to see their reaction in getting to the summit is fairly special.

We had a satellite phone: to be able to ring home was a huge thing. Dad answered the phone and I said, 'Dad, I made it. We're just sitting on the summit,' and he said, 'Oh, just one second I'll put you on to your mother,' and she goes, 'Oh, just one second I'll put you on to Karen,' and I'm going, 'Ah! Hurry up!' But everything just really worked out well.

There's all sorts of things going through your head, you know, just before you go for it, wondering what it's going to be like, the final few hours. I think the big thing is sort of fear of the unknown. We were lying there and one of the guys who had gone up the day before us came over to our tent and he said, 'Oh, so-and-so and so-and-so are stuck on the mountain.' And you're kind of sitting there wondering. Both of them got down alive anyway and they got them down the mountain safely. But the night we went for it there was actually three people died on the mountain. We passed one guy and he was really slow and really weak and you know, when we saw him I kind of thought, 'He shouldn't be up here,' but people do keep going, they push themselves. I don't know if it's some fever or what it is but he kept going and he actually made it to the summit but the Sherpas that were with him afterwards said that he turned around and he could barely walk. They had to try and support him the whole way down and they ended up being out on the mountain for about 25 hours with him before they eventually had to leave him. And that was the last that was seen of him.

I suppose you distance yourself from it to a certain extent. And it's funny, even though you see it and you know about it, you sort of convince yourself that it's not gonna be you. And it is a bit of a mind game up there as well; I guess, a mind game with yourself. If you were told tomorrow you can go somewhere absolutely brilliant you'll never have done anything that you can compare it to and you hear all the hype about it and then they say, 'But the downside is that for one in ten people, you'll never get back out of it,' you can only deal with it by thinking, 'I'm not going to be one of them. I've done the preparation. I know I can do it.'

I don't know if all this makes sense, but it's kind of hard to give a picture of what it's like up there. I can't think of anything day-to-day to compare it to, you know, to try to get it across. But that's the best I can do."

Clare O'Leary is a 32 year-old doctor from Bandon and is a daughter of one of Ireland's leading motor dealers, Kevin O'Leary. She has climbed extensively in Africa, Alaska, South America, the Himalayas, the Alps and Scotland. A member of the Irish Everest Expedition, she became the first Irish woman to reach the summit of Mount Everest.

Tadgh Philpott

"I did the Lee Swim in July 1939. I think it was one of my first competitive swims. The old course was from the Distillery Field in the North Mall to Brian Boru Bridge. At the time, you'd grease down well, and to start off, you had to dive right out into the river to turn left and go down the quays. The condition of the water was diabolical: it was an open sewer. Lots of swimmers wouldn't enter that water; quite a few of them did, but lots didn't.

The good part of it was, when you finished, there was a little wharf down the end of Brian Boru Bridge and they'd take you by the hand and you'd come up, you'd walk up Merchant's Quay and into the St Vincent's Hostel – which is gone years ago now – where you'd get a hot cup of Bovril and there were showers to try and get the muck and the grease off yourself.

At the time, it was a very, very popular swim: the crowd used to line both quays. Most of the spectators would stay on the Bachelor's Quay, Lavitt's Quay side, as it was a much better vantage point.

A lot of people were interested. Sure, if you were in a club, you'd be interested in the representative of your club, but a lot of people were interested in the competitive nature of the swim. They mightn't know one from the other, but they'd always encourage the leaders and they'd always encourage the fellas who were chasing after them. Literally thousands of people used to come out and watch. There was often more people at the Lee Swim than you'd find out in Turner's Cross in the old days, or down the Mardyke for that matter. It had a great following.

I swam the Lee Swim on a second occasion in Monkstown some years ago but it wasn't the same thing as the old Lee Swim at all. In Monkstown, the spectators were so far away that they'd hardly recognise you. In the old one, the spectators just followed you down along the quayside from the start.

Cork is a unique city in the sense that it has two channels of the River Lee: the North Channel and the South Channel. There was always more water in the North Channel than the South, because it was deeper. And how they ran the sanitary services long ago was – the cheapest you could run your service for the year was supposed to be a good thing from an engineering point of view – you ran the whole thing into the river. It was an open sewer. In the South Channel, because there was a lack of water, it used to back up. There was actually islands of, shall we say, human waste.

At the time of the Lee Swim, in retrospect, it was dangerous. If you were to go into the Lee now – to go in and pick someone out – when you're taken to hospital, the first thing you get is a tetanus injection. People used to swim there long ago and there was no protection at all other than, get Vaseline and grease your body. And that was to keep out the cold, not the rats! It was the Department of Health that condemned the Lee Swim. There were warnings about typhus, about Weil's Disease: it was a terrible bloody thing altogether. But now, with the completion of the Cork Main Drainage Scheme, they're talking about reviving the Lee Swim and I'd like to see it revived. I would like to feel that there would come a time when the Lee Swim was firmly re-established in Cork again. The river is much better now than it was back then, although there's plenty of work that still could be done."

Tadgh Philpott is one of the world's leading swimmers in the 80-84 age group. Last year, the retired union official celebrated 58 years of marriage. His current club, the Cork Masters, are reviving the historic Lee Swim as part of the European Capital of Culture celebrations in 2005.

Finbar Wright

"People in Cork have a healthy scepticism, which is important. They treat you as one of their own, as a normal human being. That's a phenomenon in Ireland anyway: while they appreciate what you do, they love the music and all that, you're not put on any kind of pedestal. That's a great thing about coming back here: being able to walk down Patrick Street. I can walk around anywhere in Cork without being hassled by anybody. While, in the US, you'd be stopped at every airport, you'd be stopped in the street. I've been accosted, even, in bookshops. You'd be hassled all the time.

I work so much in the US that I work very little in Ireland, which is unfortunate in many ways because I used love doing, particularly, the small theatres in Ireland, where there's a great intimacy with people. Places like Siamsa Tíre in Tralee, even the very small theatre in Kilworth, North Cork which I used always do when I was more based here in Ireland in the early '90s. I do miss all of that: travelling around Ireland; listening to the stories of people; people just coming backstage afterwards to chat to you. Ireland is a great country for that: there's a great friendliness here. It's part of what you are. In some way, it gets into your bloodstream, into your bones and it never leaves you.

Irish people enjoy their music and they appreciate it. The American audience is different, in the sense that they're more upfront: the number of standing ovations in any concert could be, certainly, five or six standing ovations would be no bother, because they're more effusive in their response to it. Every year, we come home: at the Point, last year, we had 7,000 people. While it's a great occasion, with the full orchestra, there's not the same intimacy there.

There's healthy scepticism, yet also a great appreciation of their own: I think that's always been a strong thing in Cork. I think we're still small enough not to take on the airs of the big cities; what they say about Paris, New York, Dublin, is that the people there think they own the world and all the rest of it. There's great industry here, great culture, although we don't have a concert hall. But even that, it's funny: it's almost as if we don't care; we're kind of saying, 'Well, the Opera House holds 1100, the City Hall roughly the same, let them come for three nights if they want to.'

There used to be a great story told about Gigli. It originates in Blackpool, actually, because the idea was that, in Blackpool, they knew more about opera than anywhere else in the world. So, Beniamino Gigli, the great tenor, came to Cork, and I think it was the Old Savoy he was in. He came out anyway and he sang his arias and everything else, and he sang as an encore, 'E lucevan le stella,' sobbed his way through it, fantastic, huge cheers and everything else. They kept calling for an encore, so he had to sing it again. 'Sing it again, we want to hear it again.' So, he sang, 'E lucevan le stella' again. Once more, huge cheers and everything else. So, he came out for a third time and they started cheering for 'E lucevan le stella' again. So, Gigli says, 'Really, I cannot go on singing it all night.' And there was a slight hush. Then, there was a voice, from way up the back: 'You'll keep singing it, boy, until you get it right.'"

Finbar Wright is one-third of the Irish Tenors. At the age of 21, he became one of Ireland's youngest priests.
He left the priesthood in 1989. He is married to Angela Desmond and they have two children.

Dr Mary McCaffrey

"I lived in Wicklow until I was eight and then we moved to Cork. I did medicine at UCC. I got involved in politics in college, about 1977, which would have been the year that Garret Fitzgerald took over as the leader of Fine Gael.

Garret had that charisma and the idea that the social agenda could be pushed from within Fine Gael was why I joined. A lot of things that we now take for granted, we would have done initial petitioning and policy documents on: like abolishing the status of illegitimacy. It was actually quite a radical group for its time if you take the whole illegitimacy thing; that was huge.

If you look at the percentage of women in businesses that make it above the glass ceiling, an awful lot hasn't changed for women. Because the structures within the workplace, within systems, haven't actually allowed it to change. And then you've got to think, well, do we need to encourage women? And I think we should because women bring a softer way of thinking that often balances out or complements the way that other people think.

Even within my own profession, the women who have made it to the top as consultants would probably have made huge sacrifices. I think as well, the importance of having women involved in different professions is that they'll often take on agendas for the sake of the agenda because it's important. Whereas often other people would say, 'Is this going to advance my career? Why are you doing it?'

I worked in the UK and I got very involved in the whole area of female genital mutilation. Ironically, the skills that I would have learned from that now help me dealing with asylum seekers and refugees in understanding their culture.

I've been very disappointed in the way we've reacted to the refugee and asylum seeker problem here – 'not in my backyard' – and yet 200 years ago we all had to emigrate as a nation. You had to emigrate. And we are now objecting to having asylum seekers and refugees in the country.

I was in the UK from '91 to '94. The troubles were quite bad in the North at the time. Being Irish wasn't particularly popular. You were definitely a 'Paddy' even if you were a doctor. And in many ways it makes it easier to understand what it's like for the people who are coming in here being rejected and sidelined.

I came back at the time of the Celtic Tiger as well – the economy was really booming, and I had great hopes that the health services would improve here. But it's getting harder and harder for staff to provide a personalised service – everyone's under pressure. Consultants are getting so much bad press for being perceived as providing a poor service. But a lot of changes that have come about in hospital systems have been driven by consultants whose agendas are purely for patient care at the end of the day.

I think we need to look at the spreading of wealth a little bit more. I mean, if you take, for example Cork. Look at the waiting list for housing. And you know, that means we have to look at how we can correct that. During the 2004 local elections in Cork, I was really disappointed at the amount of people who seemed opposed to affordable housing, social housing – without actually understanding the difference between the two. And we need to somehow examine our conscience as a nation – and locally – to see how we can become a more heterogeneous society, more accepting of other people. I think we are on the verge of becoming very selfish as a nation, if we're not careful."

Dr Mary McCaffrey is a consultant gynaecologist with the Southern Health Board. Her husband, Colm Burke, is a prominent Cork solicitor and politician: he was Lord Mayor in 2003.

Caroline Fennell

"Cork is not as impersonal as Dublin. It has a huge sense of itself. I think you find a sense of Dublin among Dubliners in various pockets. But Cork has a sense of itself as a city and there's a great sense of ownership among Cork people of their city, and of their college. I think that's really nice. That's very valuable. It's kind of a pride; it comes from a city that is a second city, but has all the sense of importance of a city, and the confidence that comes with it. As the city grows, that confidence is growing. It hasn't lead to a sort of inward-looking arrogance, I think it's becoming much more outward-looking, and European. The links that are there transnationally – between Europe, and parts of the States – are quite important: they give Cork that sense of itself. That's what's distinct about it.

I like Cork. I'm also critical of it because I feel strongly about the university and about Ireland in general. I would have been very critical of Ireland in terms of what I would have seen as a very conservative, inward-looking approach, particularly in the '70s and '80s. It strained itself to change in the '90s, and I think it has changed. That's positive. A lot of my generation would have emigrated. I was lucky enough to get a job here, so damned if Ireland could deny me, even though some of what I said at times wouldn't have sat too well with traditional, more conservative views.

I think Ireland has changed an awful lot, and I think Cork has changed an awful lot. I remember once being asked by someone, when I was speaking at a meeting in Dublin, 'You're in Cork?' And UCC to some extent had a bit of a conservative feel about it at one stage; that voices that were seen to be radical at the time would come from UCC seemed to be unusual. That has changed now.

Cork has a lot of the advantages of a smaller city, a second city. It's a good thing: it is more personal, it is a living city still; you can live and work in Cork and within half an hour, be in a totally different environment. And it's very beautiful.

It's very good from a student educational point of view too because it's so attractive. We have lots of American students who come and European students: the campus is very much part of the city and that's a huge issue and a huge attraction for foreign students. We have an American summer school starting next year. That's part of the attraction for them: not just that it's a good law school and a vibrant university, but also that there's a nice cultural dimension to their experience here.

It's not a city that is overwhelmed by its university. It's a very nice mix of a city, with lots of things going on. Cork people wouldn't be overwhelmed by anything really though. And that's something that's served them in good stead in the past and probably will again in the future.

It comes from a sense of stability maybe. They do say about Cork people that a lot of them want to come back to Cork. That has led to a sense of stability and identity, and that's important. A lot of big cities now could be anywhere; they're seriously international in that sense. Cork is international, but in a local sense. It hasn't lost its own identity."

Professor Caroline Fennell is Dean of the Faculty of Law in UCC. Born in Dungarvan, County Waterford, she studied in Cork, Canada and the King's Inns before taking a teaching position in UCC. Acknowledged as one of Ireland's leading authorities on criminal law, she lives in Kinsale with her husband and children.

Eoghan Harris

"To me, Cork is a Jewish city. It's the closest thing to a Jewish area of New York that you'll come to. In other words, it's a cockpit of struggle. Cork is not just a silven rural or urban garden city Utopia to grow up in. Cork is a cockpit even now; it's a battlefield.

I always think of Cork as being at war, and everyone is a combatant. What's at stake, literally, is your standing all the time: whether you're a 'langer' or 'sound.' And this is determined not by your intellect or your wealth or your status, but by the speed at which you move when you come under fire; your ability to take wounds; to be stoic in the face of slagging and the incredible scrutiny of character that goes on.

Cork investigates your character: it sees how you stand up under pounding. It investigates what Hemingway calls 'grace under pressure.' When they've pounded you hard enough, and you've stood up and been reasonably witty and not whinged, you're allowed respect.

My mother was from Roscommon and she couldn't deal with it. She called it 'barging.' She said she never came across anything like it in any other county. By which she meant that constant rumbustious interrogation, slagging, sardonic inquiry, and relentless aggressiveness.

To say I have affection for them would be wrong. I neither like nor have affection for Cork people. I have respect for them, and that's much more important. And in Cork, if you're dealing with them, there's no point being nice. And so, all the great Corkmen I respect take Cork on their own terms, take no quarter and expect no quarter. People like Niall Toibín, Donal Farmer, Chris Curran and Jack Lynch. They were all prepared for the kind of war which is life in Cork.

Seán O'Faoláin and Frank O'Connor are quintessential Corkmen. If you look at O'Connor and O'Faoláin on RTE programmes, you won't just notice the mellowness and the mellifluousness, you'll notice the incredible combatativeness, the readiness of soldiers who are about to be attacked at all times: they never know what quarter the attack is going to come from. So, here you see them in Dublin, relaxed, at home or in a studio, and they still have that hunch in their shoulders, because they don't know from what side the attack is going to come. They are among pussycats in Dublin and no one is going to attack them. But they still carry that Cork wariness.

What sums up Cork for me is when Kevin Costner came over here to work on a script on Michael Collins, and he was paranoid about being annoyed on the streets. I said he could walk the streets of Cork and nobody would annoy him. After an hour of this, like all film stars, he began to get worried because nobody took a blind bit of notice of him. 'Do they know who I am?' 'Yes, they do.' 'Are you sure?' So I stopped the first two – you could only call them hardchaws – that were walking along the street in very dirty trainers and tracksuits.

'Do you know who this is?' 'Of course we do…Hello, Kevin.' And he was delighted. 'C'mere, Kevin, can I have your autograph?' 'Of course.' 'Have you a bit of paper?' 'Have you a biro?' So, Costner wrote down his autograph, on his own paper, with his own pen and yer man said, 'Thanks very much, Kev, loved your 'Dances With Wolves,'" walked away and threw the bit of paper over his shoulder."

Writer and journalist Eoghan Harris spent the 15 "indelible" years in Cork between the age of five and 20. He now divides his time between Baltimore, County Cork, and Dublin.

Tony Humphreys

"You talk about a German psyche, a Spanish psyche, an Italian psyche because there are defences that are common to nations. The defence that was very common to the Irish nation was one of inferiority and that was a very clever defence. Because it would have been very dangerous for the Irish people, being oppressed by the British, saying, 'We are equal to you, we are just as good as you, we have the same intelligence, we deserve respect, we deserve to be valued.' If we had done that, as a people, we would have been annihilated even more than we were!

So, very cleverly, we doff the cap and say, 'Yes, sir, you're right, sir, we'll do that for you, sir.' It's not a weakness: every defence is a tool, it's a weapon against annihilation. The Americans developed a superiority complex, the Germans developed a superiority complex, very much in the early 1930s, following the defeat of the First World War and the humiliation that followed. Then, the Italians are much more pragmatic, histrionic and whatever. It's always dangerous to take a collective defence because each person has their own unique defences as well. But there are common ones.

The Cork psyche? Good humour - humour is very peculiar to Cork – and the put-down – Cork people are good at the put-down – but I don't see strong characteristics. I don't see strong defensive characteristics, compared to other counties. Except, there's that, 'It's the capital city,' idea. I suppose there was a little bit of superiority there, the whole notion of being in competition with Dublin. But I think that's old hat; I think that's gone by the board now.

I think Cork didn't really benefit from the boom as much as other places at all: Kilkenny, Waterford and Galway, places like that, have all had major developments since the boom. Cork didn't. In fact, it never recovered from Ford's and Dunlop's; it was such a blow to its esteem. And I think it's only in the last few years – maybe it's the whole refurbishment of the city – that the sense of pride has come back again. The city had got very dowdy and run-down. When you go around Dublin, it's very hard to find a part that you wouldn't admire, even up around the old parts of Dublin, all changed and refurbished.

I certainly feel a new spirit in Cork for the last couple of years, an emerging one. Even the fact of being the European Capital of Culture in 2005 has done a lot for Cork pride. That has motivated the refurbishment of the city that was badly, badly needed.

So, certainly, in my own business, Equinox, the jewellery shop, we've noticed a change this summer compared to last year or the year before: there's a surge of people around. Maybe people just avoided the city when it was in a state of upheaval for the last two years or so, but there seems to be a lot of people around now.

I love Cork humour. One of our basest fears is to be a failure. So, when people fall in the street, they're embarrassed, they get up very quickly and they won't make any contact with anybody. They shoot down a laneway so nobody will see them and then they'll look to see what happened to them, dust themselves down. Whereas, when a Cork fella falls in the street, 'He stays down for the compo, like. He blames the Corporation.' Cork has that little twist, it sees it in a different way. I think that's very typical Cork: we just give that twist to a normal situation."

Dr Tony Humphreys, Clinical Psychologist in private practice, author, and international speaker, lives in Lisgoold, County Cork. He is also a Specialist Lecturer in UCC and a Senior Fellow in the National College of Ireland, Dublin. His bestselling books have been translated in 25 languages.

Emma Connolly

"I remember when I was a boarder in Sacred Heart Secondary School Clonakilty convent thinking that 7am was a cruel time to be woken at. I never thought I'd work in a job that sees my alarm going off at 5.35am – and actually enjoy it. I'm in my car by 5.55am, making my way from Douglas to Academy Street. On the journey I listen to the various news bulletins to find out what's happened overnight, switching from one station to another. There's actually a whole community of early risers in the city – van drivers, street cleaners, delivery men. There's a sense of camaraderie between us all now, with lots of waving and saluting.

When I reach the office, the first job is to get a coffee, then I turn on our two radios, which are just inches from me all day; check the Press Association wire service which is constantly updated; check overnight emails; faxes; go through the morning papers; and talk to our reporters, who are in constant touch with their contacts. That allows me draw up the news list which is a menu of the day's stories. At 7.30am we have the main conference of the day, chaired by the editor and attended by all the heads of department including the Deputy Editor, Features Editor, Chief Sub Editor, Production Editor, Leader Writer and Photographic Editor. Everyone gets a copy of the news list. There is a vigorous discussion of the relative merits of the stories, where they should be placed in the paper and what should be our page one stories. After this, I allocate the stories to the various reporters and from there on in, it's action stations. The morning is measured in terms of deadlines - you have no idea how precious a 10-minute extension can be until you're a reporter trying to find vital information. It's loud, fast and constantly changing – what can start out as a page one story can become just a few paragraphs and vice versa. The end result is the Evening Echo on the streets and in the shops by lunch time. I leave the office around 3.30pm but none of us are ever 100% off, which is part of the job; news doesn't follow a schedule. If a big story breaks then we make arrangements to cover it. We have a fantastic team. There is no way I could do the job without the fabulous support I get from everyone.

It is hard working on the heart-rending stories. They put a strain on everyone. But that is part of the job, letting people know what is going on in society. But there are also the great times.
The humanity of many people is amazing; in the last two Christmases, Evening Echo readers have raised half a million euros for two great causes: the children's leukemia unit at the Mercy Hospital and Marymount Hospice. We are a community newspaper, it's outlined to you when you join our newspaper and something all of us are committed to. We, as a newspaper and as a group of people, believe in putting something back into the local community which supports us so well.

I studied journalism in Dublin City University and went to work in Mayo for a number of years. I always wanted to return to Cork and be nearer my family in West Cork. I love the tradition associated with the Evening Echo. It's there over 100 years and part of the fabric of the city – the Echo boys, the cry 'Echo! Echo! Evening Echo!' and the way the public react to our coverage of events. We sell over 28,000 copies every day and in the last few years we have won national newspaper awards for news and community coverage. It is tough and demanding job, but it is also very rewarding."

Emma Connolly is News and Fashion Editor of the Evening Echo. A native of Timoleague, she lives in Douglas and has a degree in Journalism and French from Dublin City University.

Matt Murphy

"You're very close to our maker here. I've no doubt that at times, everyone thinks about the next life. And the older I get, I think more and more about it. If you ever get doubts about the next life, or if there's a God there, you only have to look out and realise who made it. It's really something.

If you look at all the animals, and all the seaweed, and all the plants, Good Lord, someone had to make it. There has to be a Supreme Being. But nature can be so vicious: when the storms come and the seas roar, you can take nothing for granted, and you realize that you're but a speck in the whole universe. Nature, especially living on an island, it controls you.

I suppose, people would say that I'm a loner. I am. I suppose I'm nearly a total loner. I go to my own point to stand alone and think. That's where I used go when Eileen was sick. I think you're very close to God when you're standing on the rocks, looking out at the sea, seeing the power of the sea, driving up onto the rocks around you.

I would have to say, all my life, I have been a loner, and it has stood to me. Especially running a marine station. It's so solitary. It's crazy, really, what I did. My mother, God rest her, used say I was mad. She was right.

But you need the strength of being alone. You need the strength of being a loner to do what I did and to come through at the other end.

I've always said that if you do anything, achieve anything, you have to push yourself to the edge of the precipice. Make sure not to fall off, but you must go to the edge of the precipice. Both mentally and physically. And I have to say, I've done that many, many times. It isn't fun at times, when you have to do it. But if you want to survive and continue doing what you believe in, you've got to.

There's incredible peace here: I came to Sherkin 50 years ago, for a week's holidays, and I fell in love with the place. I said I'd come to live here eventually, and bought a holiday home in 1962, the same year I married Eileen. Then, we lost a lot of money in our business, and we'd no place left to go but Sherkin, and the 15 acres. We came to try it for a fortnight – came in the first week in August in 1971 – and we stayed. Our kids went to the school and we stayed.

Eileen in 1973, got cancer, but got a fabulous remission: six wonderful years. She died in 1979. She was 37. Sherkin gave me some incredible memories. I know it might sound corny, but I've no bad memories of our marriage. I was just blessed that we were living on Sherkin when Eileen got sick. That six years extra that we got, we wouldn't have got it if we were living in the rushing and the bustle.

The Lord has been great to me. The Lord has great wisdom. I have always said that the Lord giveth but he also taketh. She is still above there, minding me. The one kindred spirit I had was Eileen. She understood me. She still understands me. That's the important thing in life."

69 year-old Matt Murphy lives on Sherkin Island, where he has run an internationally-renowned marine research station since 1975. The centre attracts 16 volunteers annually from around the world to run its scientific research projects. Widowed in 1979, Matt also produces a newspaper, 'The Sherkin Comment.' His private library collection of scientific literature is the largest of its kind in Europe. Five of his seven children still live on the island.

Mercy Fenton

"Jacobs on the Mall was the perfect opportunity. We opened in December 1998. Tom McCarthy gave me a free hand in the kitchen. The local produce made the job of producing good food easy.

At the start, it was a nightmare! New staff, new restaurant, new menu, new everything! There were people, I'd say, crying going out the door because they waited so long! But that was a long time ago now.

The room is amazing. You still get people walking through the doors going, 'Oh my God, what a beautiful room, I never knew it was here.' The room still holds me in awe. It's so huge and beautiful and it's a pleasure to see it buzzing on a busy night.

I originally decided to be a chef and everyone thought I was mad, thought I was a lunatic! So, I got a job in the Devonshire Arms in Youghal, way back when I was in school. I washed dishes, made beds and waited tables for three months. I had a ball: loved the whole environment of catering and all that.

So the following summer, I worked in Seaview House Hotel in Ballylickey in Bantry, sort of as kitchen help cum chambermaid cum hanging out the washing. Anything that was required got done, but primarily, I got a chance to be in the kitchen, cooking and doing stuff.

When I finished there, I did a basic cookery course run by CERT and FÁS, a 13-week basic course. You live in a centre, you prepare breakfast and lunch for the people in the centre. I think it was about 60 to 80 of us. That incorporates the practical side of cooking, and then you'd cook the evening meal. So, it was cooking five days a week. Full of practical experience, with a little bit of theory thrown in. Then, I went back to Seaview the following summer and worked mainly in the kitchen.

My first head chef job was in Stephen Bull's restaurant in London. I was 26, which is, I suppose, average. It wouldn't be really young, but it wouldn't be really old either. I was doing alright, let's put it like that! Loved London when I was there. I shared a flat with another girl, who had been there for two years and was getting tired of it. So, we decided to go travelling for a year.

We visited South Africa, Australia, New Zealand, Hong Kong, Vietnam, Thailand and India. The best memories are from India, the smells, the colour, the people, the food, the vastness. The worst was being stuck on a train for forty hours on the way to Calcutta from Hampi.

I came back to Ireland the following December, in the late '90s. I was determined that I would stay in Cork: it's home; it's where I wanted to be long-term. If I was going to open a restaurant, I wanted to be back in Ireland, because I like it. And, in catering, your social life is very limited anyway, so you sort of need a base to start with!

There's absolutely no begrudgery. I think of Cork people always being totally fantastic, totally lovely: turning around, saying, 'Congratulations, I've followed your career for years. Well done.' Primarily complimentary. Very supportive."

Mercy Fenton (35) is Executive Head Chef at Jacobs on the Mall in Cork City Centre, and was chosen as Munster's Best Chef by Food and Wine Magazine 2004. Originally from Fermoy, she is a former British Young Chef of the Year and winner of the Roux Diners Scholarship.

Peadar Ó Riada

"We lived in a very interesting household: lots of music, and lots of people coming and going. My father refused to get a phone or any of these things, so you'd get telegrams coming to the local post office from Hollywood and places, asking for different things to be written. A stream of interesting people calling to the house all the time. And then, he just died, when I was 15 or 16.

When he died, I took over the choir. I didn't have much choice, really. He sent for me when he was on his deathbed in London and he said, 'This is what you do, this is what you do.' I hadn't done music formally up to then and I didn't study music until the following year. I was doing the Leaving Cert and I decided I was going to do music. A lot of people argued against me, trying to stop me doing it, and then I failed my Latin, so I couldn't get into university.

They came out and told me not to do music, that I was doing it for the wrong reasons. They had to pass an Act of the University Senate to change the law about the Latin for Music so I could get in…I was kind of determined to get there.

I don't regret doing music at all. It was something I was always interested in, but obviously, when I was so busy growing up, and exploring things…you take things like music for granted; you don't ever think of them as something you have to study, as it's all around you.

The act of composition, for me, is something I don't understand. If I'm writing an orchestral score, I just hear the goddamn thing in my ears as it comes along and as I write. Lots of musicians have dark periods. And particularly those who are creative musicians; they create out of nothing. Creativity doesn't come out of anything that's already existing; it's something new, a new energy that's brought into this world. And I think that people, generally, take musicians for granted: they're handy wallpaper in the background.

People who live in, for example, Dublin think it's the centre of the universe. They would be surprised to know that we think the centre of the universe is down here, in the mountains: it's not just the spiritual life, the creative life, but the quality of life. The most important thing we have is community, which is lacking in so many other places in the modern world. For example, we were at some funerals recently elsewhere in the country and were surprised at the paucity of the attendance. Whereas you go to a funeral here, and you could have thousands at it. That's dwindling in other places.

There's communion with the surroundings here. We have our own language, and our own music. I don't leave it at all if I can avoid it. It's cosmopolitan: why would I want to go anywhere else? There have always been people from other countries living here, coming here. The only thing is, that when they come here, they're all the same as everyone else. I mean, if you walk into a pub here, people won't put their arms out and greet you with a great welcome, they'll put their shoulders together, look over their shoulder and say, 'What the feck does that so-and-so want?' It takes a while for you to get in, if they accept you. But you don't just get in willy-nilly, just because you're on the scene. You've to prove that you're not a fly-by-night, airy-fairy intellectual."

Composer and broadcaster Peadar Ó Riada lives in Cuil Aodha in the Muskerry Gaeltacht with his wife, Geraldine, and their seven children. His father, Sean Ó Riada, was one of Ireland's greatest-ever composers and preceded Peadar as conductor of the Cuil Aodha choir.

"Bhí teaghlach ana-shuimiúl againn: neart ceol agus daoine ag teacht 's ag imeacht i gcónaí. Dhiúltaigh m'athair fón nó rud ar bith mar sin a dh'fáilt, mar sin gheofá teileagramanna a' teacht chuig an oifig an phoist áitiúil ó Hollywood agus áiteanna eile, ag lorg go scríobhfaí rudaí difriúla. Bhíodh daoine suimiúla ag glaoch chun na tí an t-am ar fad. Agus ansin, fuair sé bás nuair a bhíos 15 nó 16 bliana d'aois.

Nuair a fuair sé bás, ghlac mise le freagracht an chóir. Ní raibh mórán de rogha agam i ndáiríre. Chuir sé fios orm agus é ar leaba a bháis i Londain agus dúirt .' Seo a dheineas tú, seo a dheineas tú.' Níor phlé mé leis an gceol go foirmeálta roimhe sin agus ní dhearna mé staidéar ar an gceol go dtí bliain ina dhiaidh sin. Bhíos ag tabhairt faoin Ardteist agus roghnaíos ceol a dhéanamh. Mhol an-chuid daoine dom gan é a dhéanamh, agus ansin theip orm sa Laidin agus ní fhéadfainn dul chun na hollscoile. Dúradar liom gan ceol a dhéanamhl; go rabhas á dhéanamh ar na cúiseanna mí-chearta. Bhí orthu glacadh le hAcht de chuid Seanad na hOllscoile leis an riail a bhain le Laidin agus ceol a athrú agus le go bhfeadfainn dul ar aghaidh. Bhíos diongbháilte go leor dul chun na hollscoile.

Níl áiféala ar bith orm faoin gceol a dhéanamh. Bhí suim agam i gcónaí ann, ach fé mar is áil don aos óg agus iad ag fás is dócha, ní thugas aon ró-aird ar rudaí cosúil leis a bhí ann i gcónaí.
Ní rabhas riamh den tuairim gur rud é go mbeadh ort staidéar a dhéanamh air mar go raibh sé mórthimpeall orm i gcónaí.
Maidir liom féin, ní thuigim cad is brí le rud a chumadh. Más ag scríobh scór ceolfhoirneach atáim, cloisim an diabhal rud i mo chluasa agus scríobhaim de réir mar a thagann sé.

Bíonn tréimhsí duairc ag gach ceoltóir. Iadsan gur ceoltóirí cruthaitheacha iad ach go háirithe; cruthaíonn siad ón neamhní. Is rud nua é an cruthaitheacht- ní thagann sé ó aon rud gur ann dó cheana féin. Fuinneamh nua is ea é a thugtar isteach sa domhain seo agus measaim féin go nglacann daoine leis gur ann siúrálta do cheoltóirí ach nach dtugann siad dóthan aird orthu. Is páipéar-balla áisiúil sa chúlra iad.

Tóg mar shampla daoine ó Bhaile Átha Cliath. Ceapann siad gur croí-lár na cruinne é Baile Átha Cliath. Bheadh ionadh orthu a chlos go bhfuil muidne den tuairim gur thíos anseo sna sléibhte lár na cruinne. Ní hé amháin an saol spioradálta nó an saol cruthaitheach ach caighdeán an tsaoil chomh maith. Is é an pobail an rud is tábhachtaí atá againn- rud atá easnamhach go maith in an-chuid áiteanna eile sa lá atá inniu ann. Bhí ionadh orainn mar shampla, agus muid ag freastail ar shochraid áit éigin eile le déanaí, len a laghad daoine a bhí ann. D'fhéadfá dul chun sochraide anseo agus seans go mbeadh na mílte ann. Tá an traidisiún sin ag fáil bháis in áiteanna eile.

Tá rannpháirteachas leis an gceantar seo againn. Tá ár dteanga féin againn agus tá ár gceol féin againn. Ní fhágaim an áit más féidir liom é a sheachaint. Tá sé iltíreach. Canathaobh a rachainn áit ar bith eile? Bhíodh agus tá fós daoine ó thíortha eachtranacha ag teacht anseo agus ag cónaí anseo. An t-aon rud ná go bhfuil siad díreach cosúil le gach duine eile ón uair a thángadar. Má shiúlann tú isteach i dtigh tabhairne anseo mar shampla, ní fáilte 'is féile a gheofá ach daoine ag dul sa mhullach ar a chéile, ag stánadh agus ag rá 'Cad sa diabhal atá ag teastáil ón mboc sin?'. Tógann sé tamall ar dhuine socrú síos, má ghlacann siad leo. Ach ní ghlactar leat go héasca díreach mar go bhfuil tú san áit. Ní mór duit a theaspáint dóibh nach intleachtach gáifeach tú, agus go bhfuil sé i gceist agat fanacht."

Tá an craoltóir agus an cumadóir Peadar Ó Riada ina chónaí i gCúil Aodha i nGaeltacht Mhúscraí lena bhean, Geraldine, agus lena seachtar páiste. Bhí a athair, Seán Ó Riada ar cheann de na cumadóirí is fearr a bhí ar an oileán seo riamh agus b'é a bhí mar stiúrthóir ar chóir Cúil Aodha sular thit an fhreagracht ar Pheadar.

Ally Cassidy

"Even if there were no buildings here and you came and just stood on the clifftop, you look out on the whole expanse of Bantry Bay: it's quite breathtaking. So, definitely, the scenery has a large part to play in what we offer here. Also, I think the atmosphere of practice here helps: the practice that we do every day. That all contributes to the sense of peace and solitude. It creates an atmosphere where people have time to rest and reflect.

I think a lot of people come here when their lives really are in crisis and they want to make a decision about something.
It seems that a lot of people do come here when those deeper questions have begun to surface.

People come who definitely have a real interest in Buddhism, who have a real interest in exploring the teachings, particularly on compassion, so they come here to be in the environment, to attend the practices that we offer, to really explore and study the whole area of Buddhism.

Then, you'd have the people who just want to come here on holiday. I think the atmosphere here and the environment here really lends itself to quiet, to being relaxed and just having time to reflect. A lot of people just want that. And the teachings in Buddhism offer people practices and reflections. You don't necessarily have to be Buddhist for them to be really helpful in your life. I think people are really attracted to that.

The numbers over the last years have really grown, and from what I understand, in Ireland, there's a much bigger interest in Buddhism as well. People come from all over the country. People are looking for something else. In a way, to come across these teachings, it can offer you two things: it can offer you a path that you might, personally, feel quite connected to and want to follow; or it actually might reawaken your own faith. Down here, it's not that anyone is trying to convert anyone; it's often that they get a sense of their own spirituality: they read some of the teachings; they engage in some of the practices we offer; and they realise that they do have a greater sense of spirituality within them. It really helps to reconnect them with their own faith and their own belief system. That is quite incredible.

There are two elderly women who come here quite regularly, they're Catholic and they go to Mass every day. They come here to take a break from Christmas and all that hullabullo, but they're very much Catholic. One of them was saying what she got from the teachings here really enriched her own sense of spirituality and her own belief in Christ. It's quite moving when you hear people say that.

Also, we can offer it across the board; we're not saying, 'This is what we offer and you have to accept it our way.' It's very much bringing it into your own faith and tradition.

Most of the practices we do here are sitting meditation. And then, we offer courses for people who are really committed to this path. It's very, very gentle. Very simple, but very gentle. It really helps to nourish yourself and take care of yourself and treat yourself a little bit better and consequently be able to treat others a little bit better as well."

Ally Cassidy works on the Spiritual Care Programme in Dzogchen Beara retreat centre, between Castletownbere and Allihies in West Cork.

Shane Long

"It was a drunken night, to be honest with you, when we came up with the names. As the night progressed, agreement was reached. We wanted to centre everything around Cork and the names that we came out with were 'Blarney Blonde,' 'Rebel Red' and 'Shandon Stout.'

Russell Garet, our master-brewer from the US, had formulated the recipes. He had been here and he had been trying out different recipes and basically brewing stuff and throwing it out until he was satisfied. He made up all our recipes on spec, except for the stout. The stout he got down in the City Library, out of some old book. It was an old Cork recipe, a stout that was brewed in West Cork. So, he just took it off the page and brewed it.

It's all brewed here. We don't add any chemicals to our beer. It's all unpasteurised so the shelf life is fairly short, but what you're getting is potentially hangover-free beer because you've no chemicals to wreck your head...that's the story anyway, but I seem to get a hangover alright! I was told that spiel when I started – the puritans were telling me, "You definitely won't get a hangover from this stuff". I suppose, though, if you drink enough of anything you'll feel bad in the morning!

We're here nearly six years now. The first two years were really tough. It took us six months to get the licence for outside for the beer garden but once we got that, then we started marketing the festivals after the first year. They started off really small but now sometimes you're queuing from seven o'clock the two weekends of the festivals.

It's rockin' now. We're up 17% on last year, which is an awful lot. Not that I think the smoking ban made any difference here: it was just people coming here for the weather and sitting outside.

Trying to suit Cork people's taste buds is very hard. Well, we tried and then we kind of gave up. We do have a lot of Cork people drinking here but you can't even get a bottle of Budweiser in here. We took it out altogether. When the smoking ban came in we said, 'Right, we're very happy with the crowd we have here now.' What we were finding was people were coming in as the smoking ban was about to come in and they were checking the place out, the beer garden outside. And they were drinking the Smirnoff Ices and the Bacardi Breezers – not that there's anything wrong with that but we're not here to sell that. So I said, 'Yerrah, we'll take it out for a month and we'll see how we go.' So we took all of them out, including bottles of Budweiser, and we haven't had one complaint.

It goes to show that a pub can exist without them. Most people have made up their minds when they're walking into a pub what they're going to have. We've found that when we went into small pubs, we were able to sell in those pubs. We found in the big pubs – we were in a lot of big pubs – that it didn't work in any of them. And it was nothing to do with the staff not pushing it. Maybe t'was the impersonal touch; if someone comes in to a big pub they're not coming in to talk to the barman. They're coming in groups and they're doing their own thing. Every big pub we pulled out of."

Shane Long, a native of Bishopstown in Cork city's western suburbs, is the manager of the Franciscan Well pub and micro-brewery on the North Mall. 'Rebel Red,' 'Shandon Stout' and 'Blarney Blonde' are their three best-known beverages. Their two annual festivals, one each in spring and autumn, attract thousands of visitors.

Maureen Forrest

"I spent two months out there that time and I was just absolutely horrified at what I saw. One of the things that hit us all is the culture over there, which is so different, then the real plight of the people. Again, as we keep quoting, Dublin isn't much bigger than Calcutta, yet you have a population of just over a million in Dublin, and a population of 15 million that they know of in Calcutta. They have no way of counting the people in the slums. They have no birth certs: they have no idea of how many are out there.

To me then, when I saw the numbers of street children and the numbers deserted on the streets, I always felt that there was a terrible sense of destitution. They were living on the streets, they were living in the slums, with absolutely no hope of ever getting back to their villages, because they had left through dire poverty. In some cases, you had three generations of Indian people living in these slums, going back to when the British left the country. An awful lot of it was a refugee problem left by the division between Pakistan and India. Nothing was ever done about it.

And things got worse over the years. The rural areas got poorer and when people came into the cities, looking for work and looking for help that wasn't there, they just got poorer and poorer. I did feel a great sense of helplessness at what I saw there. But I came home and my priority would have been doing it for Calcutta and doing it for street children and the poor.

At night, you see the people asleep on the streets with absolutely nothing. At about four in the morning, it becomes alive, it becomes a market. Where people slept and went to the toilet the night before is then converted into a market where the people from the villages come in with all their different produce. And that goes on from about four to 10 in the morning.

Right outside our window is a butcher's stall. A guy arrives every morning with his baskets full of chickens and proceeds to decapitate each and every one of them while we're asleep, or trying to sleep, upstairs. We talk about health and safety here, and we're so particular, but he literally decapitates the chickens and dips them into the same bucket of water.

Then we have the Calcutta eagles. More like vultures than eagles. They hover over the street and they swoop down and take the heads or remnants of the chickens. That goes on then until about 11, when it actually gets so hot that the stink of the place is, not very pleasant. Just further up from that, they have a fish market, which, you can imagine, without fridges…

The support of Cork people has been absolutely amazing. We started off by having one auction in November of '98 and we raised something like £20,000. Now, over five years on, we've raised over €3m.

OK, you will get some people who say, 'Why do it for the Third World, why not do it for your own?' But I think we have wonderful people here in Cork: we have Simon, we have St Vincent de Paul, we have Share, and I think that most of the people who would query why you're doing it overseas would be the same people who wouldn't be doing a lot themselves."

Maureen Forrest has been involved in Third World charity work, both as a volunteer and a fundraiser, for over 20 years.

After a visit to Calcutta in 1993, she and two others, Celena Daly and Edith Wilkins, decided to found the Hope Foundation.

The charity runs several homes in Calcutta, reaching out to around 5,000 street children.

Mary Johnson

"There's an arrogance in Cork that excludes entry. There's not the pride that there should be. Frank O'Connor is such an obvious example. Seán O'Faoláin is another. Living with Patrick Galvin has been an experience in many ways. He's a multi-talented man, he's a self-made man, but he wouldn't have made it in Cork. He made it in England. He came back to Cork about six times, but he walked away every time. It was like being absorbed into a nothingness when he came back. O'Connor tried to come back, tried to live with it, but felt stifled and had to go away again.

I met Patrick Galvin as a playwright. He's written about nine plays and they're all brilliant. Controversial, I have to say, all the time. Censored, all the time. Paddy had a stroke in February and one of the ideas was that he and his plays would be honoured. I went to the powers-that-be two or three times – in between looking after Paddy – and I got this mealy-mouthed answer back. He's regarded as brilliant but dangerous.

And he's still there. People are treating him as if he's gone away, but Paddy Galvin is still there. He's improving. He's not back to himself yet, but he's about 80% back. Physically, he's paralysed on one side, but we're talking about his whole being. Everyone came to see was he going to die or was he not. When he wasn't going to die, we haven't seen anyone since. It's amazing! I'm actually quite tired at the moment, but we're getting by, we're rising up again.

I was never one to say, 'No.' Bureaucracy is there to be tested all the time. I'm getting older and it's getting harder, but, even at university, I used to write reams and reams of stuff about how things were done badly. They asked us to write an appraisal of the careers' service when we graduated. I wrote six pages back to them! All along the line, I've been testing it all the time. But you just have to test it. Bureaucracy is set up as a block to people and it's that kind of thing that absolutely befuddles people who are struggling, people in economically marginalized areas. That finishes them. It destroys you as a person.

The last time we went up to the Arts' Council, we were asked had we a TD in our area that we could lobby. 'Jesus Christ,' I thought, 'this is what the Arts' Council was set up for!'

The bureaucracy is hard to get over. That's one thing, but I find that there's a block also, maybe a mental block. If I were to compare Cork with Kerry, I would say that Kerry knows how to nurture its people and if they have any talent, they shout about it. And they document it, and they boast it, and they celebrate it. Cork mainly brushes it under the mat.

I think it's post-colonial. That's the only thing I can think. I don't think the British really got into the pockets of Kerry: it has been untouched by real colonialism.

Even in Cork, if you go outside Macroom, you're into the Gaeltacht area – the British didn't go there because of the mountains – you have a language and you've a real pride in your identity.

Cork's brilliant, full of creativity, if you've no real ambition to be nationally, or internationally, focused: you can really go places within a small pool, but, if you try to raise your head above it, I'm not sure that you'd be helped. Maybe it's the same with all places: hard to know!"

Mary Johnson, who was born and raised in Northern Ireland, is married to the writer Patrick Galvin. They have been together for 30 years, 15 of which have been spent in Cork. Mary was also the founder of the Munster Literature Centre.

Dave Barry

"I'll tell you about the day I got kicked out of a County Cork Church. I was told by the bride and groom that the priest didn't allow any photographers inside in the church. So, it meant that we couldn't have any photographs at the ceremony, even though all the photographs we took the marriage ceremony were all from behind anyway, as we couldn't even get onto the altar, in those days. But I thought that I would do something nice for the bride and groom. So, when the Mass had started, I went up to the balcony of the church, I set up my camera on the tripod and just waited for the moment.

The parish priest, who was marrying the couple, was going through the responses and, for some reason, he just looked down the church and saw me up on the balcony.

So, in the middle of marrying the couple, he puts his hands out and he just brushes them aside and he marches down the aisle. He caught my by the scruff of the neck and kicked me out the door with his boot! I was in an awful state, afraid to go back into the church. Photographers always went into the sacristy for the signing and the next thing I knew, one of the altar boys came around and said that the parish priest had said that if I wanted to take a few photographs, I could go in. I went in, took a photograph of the signing of the register and in fact, I took the photograph and I asked the parish priest did he want to stand in for a photograph. And he said, 'Yes'!

The bride and groom explained to me afterwards that, two years earlier, her sister was getting married. A photographer came up at the ceremony, left off the flash, and the parish priest ordered him out. That would be going back to 1965 or 1966 now, which makes what happened next quite unusual.

The photographer turned around and said to the parish priest, 'I'll look after my job and you look after your job.' With that, the parish priest waltzed over the altar rails, went to give him a box and the photographer went to duck, slipped, banged his head off the seat and was knocked out cold. He'd to be carted out by some of the guests.

He looked for an apology first off the parish priest, which he didn't get. He went to the Bishop of Cork, who was Dr Cornelius Lucey at the time, and made a formal complaint, which didn't get anywhere at all. So, then, he commenced civil proceedings for assault. The case fell – never went to court – because he couldn't get one solitary single person to come as a witness. No one would ever dare stand up in court against the parish priest. But, the priest still thought that photographers were bad, bad news.

I made up for that when I saved the late Father Charlie Lynch. I was at a wedding in the Honan Chapel and I was at the side, waiting for the exchange of rings, when, next thing, my eye was caught by a flash of light. His vestments had gone up against a candle, they had caught fire and because of the special substance that's used in the cleaning of the vestments, it was just, PSSSSHHHH. I just made a grab for him – the people in the church didn't know what was going on – and I started beating the hell out of him. 'In the name of God!' he was shouting. He didn't realise he was on fire. But we all got out alright."

David Barry is a well-known Cork wedding and social photographer. He founded Barry's Photographic in 1967 in Patrick Street and the business is now based in Pembroke Street. He is a Peace Commissioner. He has been involved in the scouting movement for over 35 years and is presently County Commissioner.

Vivienne Roche

"I suppose, from my era, art as a career would not have been an option. I wouldn't have known many artists in my childhood. And you just wouldn't confront much art, as opposed to now, where of course there definitely is a lot more art in people's everyday experience. But I always did love drawing and painting as a child.

I think I vaguely planned to be an art teacher: there was no question of becoming an artist. I went to the School of Art, now know as the Crawford, but for a purpose that was other than simply making art. Very quickly I knew I wasn't going to teach for the rest of my life. And even though I did whatever exams were necessary for teaching, I just really felt that being in art school was quite broadening and it could prepare me for something else. And I had quite a technical art education, which was very valuable. It was a very, very broad curriculum, because the purpose of it really was to teach, and so to teach at different levels and to be able to teach anything to do with art. So that's how it was taught and that's very broadly: dabbling in lots of things, until you got a feel for what you liked.

Maybe sculpture was interesting in Cork because there was a great teacher, John Burke, in the college at that time and so there was this dynamic feel around the sculpture department. He was young, he had been in college in England after he had been in the School of Art, and he introduced us to what was going on in Britain at that time, which was very strong.

I think the year that I went to the School of Art – I may be wrong about this – that between the whole of the three years ahead of us, that there were 16 people in the school: there were very few role models, there were very few people working. So maybe it was an exciting time: it was a time when students were active; shaping their own education; feeling that they could.

In the last few years I really have noticed that I feel much more like a county person. Cork as a city is fairly incidental. That's quite interesting and maybe it coincides with the fact that the seascape has entered my work over the last seven years. So I'm very contentedly working here.

But, I'm in Dublin more often than I'm in Cork these days, so I'm not lacking in urban experience! And at the moment I'm working on a project where I'm in London every fortnight, if not most weeks, so cities have always been a part of my life. You don't have to be in the experience of a city to know what a city is about. I suppose I do feel like I have the best of both worlds in that I can work from a quiet environment here that stimulates me: the actual physical environment stimulates me, and at the same time I can have urban experiences as I wish as well.
The downside of that is the to-ing and fro-ing all the time, but it's well worth it.

You know, maybe for some years I would have worked in quite an isolated way here, which I felt wasn't that healthy so I welcome that I'm working with other people and buzzing backwards and forwards to wherever those projects might be. I have a good base here but yet my working life is actually in different places."

Vivienne Roche is one of Ireland's leading sculptors. Born in Cork in 1953, she studied at the Crawford College of Art and at the School of the Museum of Fine Arts, Boston. She has exhibited in France, Finland, Sweden, England, Germany and the US. She lives in Garretstown, County Cork.

Fr Tom Hayes

"In terms of how Cork began, I suppose there is a small bit of a conflict between the historical purist and people who follow the religious tradition. Because it's extremely difficult to get a precise history of St Finbarr, a lot of the historians will challenge the beliefs of the people in regard of the establishment of the city and the traditions of St Finbarr. It now appears as if he may actually have come from Ulster originally!

However, there isn't any argument or dispute about the fact that much of contemporary Ireland – and much of contemporary Europe – grew up around historical religious centres – in many cases monasteries. That would be true of a lot of the major cities and the little towns, in our neighbouring island as well as continental Europe. It's clear that's what happened here, because the centres of religion were also the centres of education, they were the centres of trade and commerce, they were the centres of learning, the centres of craft, where a lot of skills were passed on and honed.

And from the early days, the heart of Cork city is connected with the faith of the people, the 'God question' of the people, and the 'God search' of the people who lived in the marshland. Down through history, that tradition would have been continued on by some very significant people, who would still be very much associated with Cork – for example, Nano Nagle. She created a major milestone in the education history of this country by establishing a school in Douglas Street around South Presentation Convent. She was from a wealthy family in North Cork, she was educated on the continent and the pattern of the time would suggest that she had a career ahead of her, or that she would have married a member of the nobility or, at the least, a member of a wealthy family.

She decided to step out of her traditional role and instead became a religious sister and she established her own community in Cork. She fed the children of the poor and educated them.
She was one of the first people in Ireland to acknowledge that the key to progress is education; in recent times, what people are saying about the Celtic Tiger is that the key to the boom in the past decade was having a well-educated population to take advantage of the international circumstances. Nano Nagle would have seen that in the late 1700s and early 1800s. She saw that, when Cork was in a dreadful state at that stage, if there was to be a chance for the people to progress, they had to be educated.

There would be a similar tradition in Cork with, for example, the Presentation Brothers and the Christian Brothers and, also, different bishops down through the history of this Diocese would have brought different religious communities to Cork, particularly over the last two centuries.

Whatever part of the city you stand in, or walk in, there is a connection with some religious community, some community of faithful, that worshipped in a nearby spot through the centuries. A lot of these sites are now blended into the architectural past: some of the very old churches, for example, and, in particular, the Red Abbey, just south of the river, which is one of the very old remains of a believing community. But wherever you go, there are such examples: the faith story of this city is very much alive: it's in the buildings and in the people."

Fr Tom Hayes is a native of Drimoleague. He studied in Spain, Maynooth and Wisconsin USA. Ordained in 1985, he is Diocesan Media Director. He is also Chair of the Diocesan Pastoral Strategy Group for the Cork and Ross diocese.

Robert Splaine

"Ah, you'd have good days and bad days. Sometimes you'd get fed up of it because it's very time consuming, you know, seven days a week: it's 52 weeks of the year. There are no holidays for horses really. They don't understand when it's Christmas Day, Sunday, Bank Holidays; they still have to be looked after. So it's a very time-consuming job but it has its rewards.

There's a great satisfaction if you find a horse and something tells you – your experience plus intuition – that, 'This is a good horse.' But it takes six or seven years before you may actually realise that you're right. There's always that, 'I wonder am I right…but I think he is…and that was good what he did today.' And next week you do something and next month or maybe in six months' time. It's a progression that you have to be very careful with because, if you make the wrong move, you can spoil the horse. So, it takes a lot of time, but it is very satisfying to see the raw material mature into something very, very good.

Because it actually gets you up in the morning, really. Who would want to get up on a rainy morning when everybody else is in bed and get out and work with something? It's making the dream happen, really, you know? And that side of it is very rewarding. They're not all stars, you know. Your horse shouldn't have to be a star. A lot of people like just a nice horse who's well-schooled and can compete at a certain level. It doesn't have to be international potential. It just needs to be a decent, hard-working, honest horse.

I've often thought, 'Why bother?' But I think all those little ingredients make it quite an interesting, complex mix that keeps you thinking. And you're never short of a challenge, you know? And you're always short of that little bit of knowledge. You want to know a little bit more.

So, it keeps you out there and doing it and finding out little bits and pieces, because you never know where you'll find the answer. Maybe it won't be the answer that you want, but once you get to that stage, you'll know whether you were right or wrong. I think that once you've finished learning, sure, you might as well give it up then. A horse will teach you something every day.

One thing I've learned is that the more you put in, the more you will get back. You have to treat them with discipline, yes, of course. You have to be firm and you have to know how to speak their language, in a way. If they don't trust you, then you can't expect them to do what you want them to do. And there has to be great trust and a great bond because you're actually asking them to do something quite unusual.

I mean, it's big poles, very high. Why jump it? What's it all about? There has to be a bond and there has to be great loyalty between man and beast to jump as one in the ring. And any day that I've had great success, I can always look back and say, 'It wasn't a fluke that it happened.' On that day there was something special going on. And you rarely win something big by fluke. It takes a gradual, very careful preparation. And when it works, it's fantastic. When it doesn't, you just have to move on."

The renowned showjumper Robert Splaine runs the Coolcoran Stud in Belgooly, County Cork.

Gill McAllister

"The work here is that you're an advocate, a support; they accept you and welcome you to their homes. Once you're straight and honest, genuine and fair, the community accepts you then for whoever you are, once they know you've their best interests at heart.

It was 1994 before this Project opened and other community projects were then set up. There was very little in place before that, except for the Family Centre. The local community guards, the teachers, the priests were instrumental in setting up the projects and services we've got here.

There are 64 projects funded by the Department of Justice nationally and eight of them are in Cork city and county. We all have the aim, basically, of preventing young people from getting into crime. How we interpret that very much depends on the needs in our community. The work has always been seen as a co-operative approach between the Gardai and the project workers themselves, trying to improve community relations.

Our project works in two ways. Our primary way of working is with what we call our 'core group' of young people: they're 12 to 18 years of age. We work with them to prevent them from getting into crime or divert them from crime. They would have been referred to us by the Gardai, schools, or at this stage now, young people are referring themselves, or are being referred by their friends. At any one time we work with 35 young people in that category. The majority of them are boys and we work with them for a minimum of a year. We start in September and set up small groups of six. We work with them after school and they do a combination of a group work programme and activities. There is always a minimum of two staff for every group session we run, so they get a lot of time and attention. The group work is challenging behaviour: giving them useful information about drugs, alcohol, sex education; giving them all the basic tools to help them develop. Broadening their horizons too: a key focus is challenging their attitude towards the Gardai, towards crime, towards life in general. The activities then are the fun part, day trips and so on. Today, they're down in Kinsale, canoeing.

I've been here a long time, and a few of the staff are from the area, so we have really good local knowledge. We're right in the heart of the community, so they can drop in any time and have a chat. And the fact that there's only six in the group means that they have a really close bond. Every time they've come in, it's, 'How are you getting on in school?' 'How did your match go last night?' Really checking in and building close bonds with them. They enjoy that, but I don't think they could put words on that themselves. But you see that: the attachment they form. We visit homes and schools too to check in. At the end of the year, we review the young person's attendance, their commitment, their need to stay on for another year. A year is a short time, so generally, if they want to stay on for another year, they do. That's the main part of our work.

Then there's also our outreach work, which is providing services to the whole community, this includes the regular indoor soccer and weekend open sessions, as well as the eight-week Summer Programme. It's also a way of meeting young people who should have been referred to us who haven't been and just raising our profile in the community all the time."

Born in Kent and educated at university in Liverpool, Gill McAllister came to Cork – her mother's hometown – in 1994, initially working in drug treatment, before going on to take a diploma in Youth and Community Work in University College Cork. She lives in Berrings, County Cork, with her husband.

Kevin O'Shea

"My Dad had a hardware store. Charleville was a very different place to what it is now. Very little affluence. And the customer was very important, totally different to what it is today. He was obviously making a living out of it, but it was helping people too: Christmas Eve and farmers coming in to pay their bills and having drinks. That's my memory of it.

I studied for the priesthood for four years. I left to see the other half of the world, I think. But what was interesting about being in the seminary was, it was the first place that I was in a play. I was fascinated by all of it. I found I had kind of a whole dream or make-believe world. The first play that I ever acted in there was, 'Home is the Hero,' by Walter Macken. And I really got a bad bug from there.

When I left there, I worked in my dad's shop for a while. Then I did a bit of travelling; I'd say I was a hippy for a while. I did every kind of job. What kept me in Ireland, even though I did leave it every now and then, was hurling. I think sport is wonderful. People can be at their very best in sport. I would have hurling as a tourist attraction, no question about it. You have people going to Spain to watch the bull-fights; I think the very essence of Irish people is in a hurling match. And I think sport transcends the ordinary. If you were at the All-Ireland hurling final or a club final and there's two minutes to go and it's a draw and you owe the Credit Union €14,000, you wouldn't worry about it too much.

But I got a reasonably permanent job. You meet someone, and that changes your life…so I started to get serious about work. I started off as a labourer on a building site in Mallow and I was supposed to be there for seven or eight weeks, but I ended up staying for seven years. Then, when I got the Credit Union job, I definitely had to get serious about life.

I think the spiritual is very important. That's why I think theatre is important. I think it's the one place – other than a church or a monastery – where you take off for yourself on your own. I think it's possible with theatre to create a magical place, where real values are precious, where the truth is valuable. And I'm not trying to intellectualise here: I think primarily theatre is there to entertain, but it has also got the possibility of elevating all of us. It can colour and shape your life. And that's what really interests me about theatre. It is possible – and not alone possible, but happens every now and then – that something precious, something unique, in that moment is created. That kind of space, where everything is possible, can happen in a theatre. And that's why I love doing it.

Servicing people is the core of the Credit Union, that's why we're there. We're an organisation of members. And our job is to service the members. If enough of them wanted driving licence application forms, we should be able to do it. My job is to help other people. You need common sense and to realise how ordinary you are. That's very important. We're all vulnerable. We need others. I can't do a play without all of the cast, without the people who build the set, paint the set, who light it, who do front of house. So, I am nobody without them. And you wouldn't want to forget that."

Kevin O'Shea is the manager of the Credit Union in Charleville. He founded the Shoestring Theatre and Arts Club, with which he is still heavily involved. He lives in Newtownshandrum with his wife, Patricia, and Aoife.

Liam Cashman

"This spin and spin and spin promotion on the TV now is the start of another gambling crisis in the UK: not today, not tomorrow, but in 20 or 25 years if they keep promoting it like this. It's absolutely nonsensical. You're not allowed to have a cup of tea or read the paper or anything: it's just, 'Get in and put your money on the spin, put your money on the spin.' There's a spin every 10 seconds. The odd auld punt is quite healthy, the same way as an odd pint is healthy, but having 12 of them is unhealthy. In moderation, in moderation.

We would be traditional bookmakers in that sense. We want people to use their judgment and study it, and get a bit of satisfaction out of having a win rather than gambling as such. Couldn't see any benefit in that, gambling on that spin of ball. Nonsense.

Late in '73, maybe early '74, I opened our first betting shop in Blarney Street. We bought that office – there were another couple of chaps involved at that stage – off John Paul Curtin and then we opened another office in Sheares Street. And the office in Maylor Street then. I think they all opened around the same time.

I'd worked in the offices in England for 12 years. I had it in my mind to open up back here. Whether it would work out or not was another matter entirely. The betting offices were a new thing in England. Service was quite basic here. No morning prices, there was only ante-post on two or three races: the National, the Lincoln and the Cambridgeshire. Real, real basic. In our office, we started displaying all new things like in England. Most people didn't know what you were doing. But down on Maylor Street there, there was a load of dockers who had been to England and they loved it. They loved being able to take a price and so on like that. They appreciated it and the service improved away over the years.

We've 10 shops now, six in the city. We've a telephone service, a website. It's just an information site for now; you can just check prices at the moment. We hope to go on Aertel soon.

We have adapted. You have to adapt. Everything evolves. We haven't expanded hugely. We try to concentrate on quality rather than quantity. Our managers and relief managers are directors of the company. We are more like a co-operative in a way. All the managers and relief managers plus the principal staff of all the branches of the company meet at least quarterly and discuss the ways and means of improving the business and any other thing they need to talk about. Discussing, introducing things, cutting off lines that are no longer popular, things like that. You're getting your feedback then from the ground. All those directors work in shops, they have ongoing experience of working in shops and what the customer requires.

I'd be very concerned with that spin and win type thing. I hope the Irish don't follow. The English are trying to make themselves the gambling capital of the world. I don't know who's doing the thinking for them; I certainly wouldn't like Ireland or Dublin to be the gambling capital of the world. That means you're taking over from Las Vegas, and if you can get more impersonal than that, then you're fair impersonal."

Liam Cashman is chairman and director of Cashman's Bookmakers. Born outside Killeagh in East Cork 61 years ago, he emigrated to Britain and worked for 12 years as a bookie after betting shops were licensed in 1961. He then returned to Ireland in 1973.

Mary O'Sullivan

"I suppose society at large would look at the travelling community as having no expectations of us as a community. The government would certainly have no expectations of us as Irish citizens.

I'm a member of the Cork Traveller Women's Network. One of the women came up to me and she said, 'This fella phoned from the City of Culture.' We set up a meeting and he more or less said to us, 'Look, we want you to generate an idea. Put it on paper. Bring it back in to us.'

One of the women said, 'Would we build a wagon?' I met this girl, Marie O'Shea, and she is fantastic. She sat down with us and listened – really listened. She wrote up a proposal. The man from City of Culture looked at it and said it would have to go to the directors.' So we had to wait a week. He rang that evening and said, 'It looks like we're building the wagon!' So the project started.

We're actually six months into it. We're at stage one, the wheels, the sides are up and they're just starting the barrel top. We have traveller men actually building it. One of the men, John Carroll, would have built them as a trade years ago. And the other man, James, has really good skills in welding and stuff like that.

January to December is the time frame for the project. We're linked into all the groups across the city, the women's groups. We're going to have a shawl, we're going to have a skirt, we're going to have the old pinnies. I remember the pinnies. I remember my mother used actually wear one of them. And paper flowers. Beautiful now! They're crepe paper but they are identical to a flower. The skills that are within the community are not lost. They're being tapped into. The men are doing the structural work. The women are going to be doing the interior design of, like, the curtains, the material that'll go on the roof of it, the paper flowers.

The museum in Fitzgerald Park will house the wagon. That will mean the children can see a piece of their cultural heritage built by traveller men, decorated by traveller women.

I can't believe what this project has opened up. And the great interest and impact it has had as a project on the community. I've seen traveller men shaking their head and saying, 'Where did I ever think that I'd ever live to see the day that 35 years after the last one was built that a project like this would be underway?' The support that we've had through the Culture Capital and the Sculpture Factory – that's where it's being built – is phenomenal.

We've brought the Older Traveller Women's Group in to see the wagon as it's being built. You're regenerating a whole cultural thing. They're housed now but you're giving them a flashback. One of the women said, 'Can you imagine rearing eight children in a wagon?' Stuff like that. And it's really, really bringing back memories.

But for them physically to be able to climb three steps and walk in. And see exactly what their mothers, fathers, grandparents actually lived in. And were part of. It's just amazing. People are just saying, "Can I give you something to display in the museum

So I'll be fairly busy now finishing the wagon – well, the men will – and preparing for the St. Patrick's Day parade. It'll be interesting to see what reaction it gets in the parade. Because I was sitting there one day and I was saying, 'Hmm…we're viewed so negatively…'"

Mary O'Sullivan is a widowed settled traveller and a member of the Cork Traveller Women's Network. She lives in Douglas.

Gerry Murphy

"Churchtown is a planned village, rebuilt between 1830 and 1850. The original settlement goes back well over 1,000 years when it was called Brugh Thuinne. Lewis's 'Topographical Dictionary of Ireland,' refers to Churchtown and its population of nearly 3,000 in the early 1830s.

By 1997, when I came back to Churchtown, having been away since 1972, the population of the village had dwindled to about 70 or so and there was a lot of dereliction and empty houses.

Up to 1997, I had worked in financial services, mostly in Dublin. I became somewhat disillusioned with financial services at that time and resigned to do my own thing, largely centered on the revival of Churchtown, which I saw as an opportunity to create a lasting legacy. I have been involved in other business ventures since 1997 but mostly I've been in Churchtown or around Churchtown or thinking about Churchtown!

Originally, back in 1997, when we set up the Churchtown Village Renewal Trust we set out a seven-year plan to 2005. I think we have completed about 80% of the plan, which is very satisfying. Back in 1997, when we had our first meeting in Churchtown, I don't think anyone believed that what we were planning was possible.

Since 1997, I have devoted, I suppose, 70% of my time to Churchtown and its revival. I've used other projects, wherever they have been successful, to fund what's been happening in Churchtown. But, by now, I'm glad to say we're over the hump: Churchtown has made it. It's not loss-making any more.

And that in itself is a great achievement. Churchtown village will never be a really big place but there'll be 500 people by 2010 and it may grow somewhat beyond that. The actual parish itself had a population of about 650 in 1997 with the vast bulk living outside the village. By 2010 the parish should have a population of 1,200.

The late '90s were good for property development, which definitely helped get Churchtown going. But then we had to create a belief in Churchtown so that young couples would to want to live here: we have been very successful, with over 70 new families now living in the village and as many again due to arrive in the next five years. Back in 1997 people said, 'No-one will ever buy a house here.' The cynics were convinced that it was an exercise that would end in tears. But it hasn't! Property prices in Churchtown have taken off substantially: the houses that we were selling two years ago are now worth €50,000 more to the people who bought them.

I see money as a tool. That is just my opinion of course and this philosophy is not for everyone. I am happy to make money and to use that money to make things happen, not to store it up or hoard it. I like the notion of using money as an agent of change. If I have money I try to make it work, to do things. And I'd like to think that most of the things I do – because I'm far from perfect or right – would be good for the community overall.

Of course, development can create inconvenience. And whenever you try to do anything, when you raise your head to do things, you inevitably upset other people. I accept this as a reality and try not to dwell on the negative comments. So overall, I'd prefer to be judged, not so much on my activities, but on my results. And I think the result, in 2010, will be a really special village."

As a teenager, businessman Gerry Murphy left Churchtown, near Charleville in North Cork, to go to boarding school.

In 1997, he returned and founded the Churchtown Village Renewal Trust. He divides his time between his home in Dublin and

Churchtown. In 2001 he was presented with the 'Cork Person of the Year' award for his rural renewal work.

Liam O'Regan

"I had gone to UCD and a printing course in London, so I had a reasonable background in English and printing and everything else. I was only 22 when I became editor but the paper badly needed a kick in the ass, and it needed somebody who wanted to bring in modern methods.

It was very backward, in terms of legibility, and also in terms of pagination. We had, maximum, 20 pages. Now our pagination is about double that. The printing process was very laborious and the result wasn't great. So, we were one of the first papers in the country to change over to offset printing in 1975.

Our printing press runs at about 16,000 an hour. The other machines did 3,000 an hour. We print the paper in two or three sections, and the print run is only an hour and a half, whereas the old machine would take a whole day to print.

It had to happen. The demands for a bigger paper were there, but it was the poor printing standard really, more than anything else. Advertisements weren't printed well. Just bad printing. If it hadn't happened, we'd have closed, no doubt about it, even though my father opposed it at the time. But he lived long enough to see it was the right decision. Every other paper followed. There's no paper left now printing by letterpress, as far as I know, in this country.

The emphasis is local all the time, more so than a daily, which strives to be international. The irony of it is that the 'old' Southern Star, which was founded in 1889, and the Skibbereen Eagle in 1857, tried to be international because the rural people then couldn't buy the daily papers: they were too expensive, something like three and four pence, which was enormous.

We would be a nationalist paper. We were founded, ironically, by the clergy, to counter the Protestanism of the Eagle. But then Sinn Féin booted out the clergy, and eventually, my father booted out the whole lot of them. Well, he just took them out really, one by one.

I write the paper's editorials, and I've been doing it for years. It's of vital importance. You feel you must try and inform the public rather than just give a superficial gloss-over. Very few weeklies now bother their heads with editorials, just a few throwaway remarks. I think that's a poor reflection on the newspaper industry. There are serious issues, like the referendums on things like the EU Constitution, abortion, divorce. People need a lead; whether it's wrong or right, it's an effort anyway.

I'd hope that a family member would come in and take over, and I'd be there to help. And it should have happened before now. But until one of them does come in, I'll have to keep going. I don't want to sell the place. I think only 12 out of 50 weeklies in Ireland haven't been gobbled up at this stage.

The locals prefer a locally-owned paper. I think they do anyway. There's a history in all these places. It's kind of sad for the independent weekly press that they're being bought out. Maybe the readers don't care, but, it's like if you go into a shop, you like to meet the owner. A lot of people do anyway, in small towns. Maybe not in the city, but in a town like here, people like to meet the guy who's running the place, because he's usually more attentive. But maybe it doesn't apply to media. I don't know."

At 22 years of age, Liam O'Regan took over the editorship of the Southern Star, the famous weekly newspaper based in Skibbereen, County Cork. Now 67, he has been editor for nearly half a century. His father had been a director of the company since 1919, before assuming a full-time role in the 1940s. In 1939, the Star bought out the Skibbereen Eagle, which is now incorporated in its title and presumably still keeping an eye on the Tsar of Russia.

Fiona Turley

"There was a course on here in the old Market House in Kilworth. Postgraduate: people would spend a year here working on a product or working on ideas for business. The people from the Crafts' Council would have been coming up to the college in Belfast and promoting that course. That's how I arrived in Kilworth.

It was a welcoming place. I would imagine a good 10% of the people who came through that course over the years stayed in Kilworth. It's incredible. I've a friend I went to college with who's still here. So, there was something about Kilworth. And then, I suppose, a very tall handsome husband.

Kilworth is a lovely village, it's a very open village. They'd be very welcoming to anyone who comes into it. It's very good, a good place to live. Everybody chooses different paths, but when you find yourself living somewhere, then you must make it good there.

You had students from art college – they're not your ordinary type of student, shall we say, still under the whole influence of art college – who didn't look the same, never mind walk or talk the same. So, especially for a very quiet village, the people were just unbelievable. Very open. There were houses made available for rent at a time that people didn't rent houses out. It took a lot of work to set the course up here, and it was a terrible shame that it left and went to Kilkenny, because every year, there was 10 or 12 people from all over the country coming to live here and experiencing the people here, but also, the people here experiencing them. It was fantastic.

Most people coming down here at the start were shell-shocked; it was just completely different. None of us had cars, we had no money, so we had to stay here. You socialised in the pub. Very, very different to Belfast! But I'd say there's very few who ended up not missing the place. And the amount of people that have stayed is absolutely incredible. And a few people married local people from here and moved back to where they were from. It was like an early dating agency! There must be something about the place.

You meet amazing people coming in every day, from all over the world. A couple of weeks ago, a woman came in from Fairbeach in Florida. Sure that's just incredible. That happens all the time.

I'm very open to things. If someone comes in and asks, I'll say, 'Yes.' I don't ask anything about money or about contracts: I just trust that everything will flow as it naturally should. I don't get too fussed over the big things. I've been out to Belarus to paint the walls of an orphanage. I did up the décor in a pub in Hungary. I've also done work with SeaWorld in Florida. I'd paint anywhere.

When I was younger, I had other opportunities: I could have gone to London; I could have gone anywhere. I was trained in textile design, and that's based in London and Milan; that's probably where you'd have to go. And I thought that's where I was going. But I just take things as they come, though determined to make something of them. I think because I'm open to things happening that they happen. I think memories of things in life are as important as money. And I've lots of those. I've been in a lot of strange places with art. The story would be more interesting than the bank balance!"

Textile artist Fiona Turley grew up in Seaport, near Newcastle, County Down. She attended college in Belfast and originally came to Kilworth in North Cork to do a postgraduate degree. She has lived there ever since, with her husband, Noel O'Brien and their two daughters. Her craft shop and gallery is situated at the edge of the village.

Patrick Annesley

"When I was a child, life in houses like this one was still in some ways clinging on to the Edwardian period. A lot of things were done on site. You had a permanent carpenter, for example. Everything you go to the Co-op for now – well, not everything, but most things – were produced here in an earlier era. So, much of the goods and services you now have to buy in, as it were, were just part of the everyday life of the place. All that has changed. A house of this size, in this day and age, is more a worry than a pleasure, to be frank.

We don't get many visitors by tourism standards. We're a bit too off the beaten track, I think; this isn't a good stopping-off point, really. So, we'd get something like 4,000 visitors and divided out over the months that we're open, that isn't a lot. We'd like to get more, but I wouldn't like the garden to turn into a garden which exists just to attract visitors. It must retain its character. I think what Annesgrove represents is a style of garden which happened a lot in the end of the 19th century and the start of the 20th century in parts of Scotland and Wales and the south-west of England.

And these gardens need not just to be a bit wild – that happens whether you like or not, of course! – but they have to keep a sense of being quite secretive places. If you lose that, in the end, you start designing a garden to accommodate the visitors.

An earlier period of formal open-landscape gardening – ornamental gardens – envisaged people as part of the scenery almost. And, of course, in the 18th century, landscapes were quite busy: there were far more people engaged in working on the land in those days. But these late 19th century wild gardens were meant to be a bit mysterious and a bit secretive – almost to be an improvement on nature – and look as though men didn't have much to do with them. So, you'd spoil that if you put in wide paths and clear signposts and lots of handrails.

It takes time to realise that, with a garden which has been created very largely by one person – my grandfather – it takes time to disentangle the principles, or the important things involved, from the lesser things. When it comes to think about how to preserve it or maintain it, you almost have to pick a moment in recent history and decide that's the way you wish to keep it. That's what it took time to realise here: that while you had to keep the garden going, we had to maintain its identity. It makes things easier in a sense, because we don't feel compelled to pay any regard to the fashions of the moment at all.

I suppose the preoccupation is to try and keep the place together, to maintain the garden. The livelihood is based on farming, which is a precarious source of income, these days. So, we are stuck with the problem of trying to get sufficient means to keep things going. An enormous amount of the gardening is done by students here on work experience, which is a solution. It's great for them and it's very good for us, but it means you are constantly struggling to keep a sense of continuity.

It's now difficult to see a long-term future in farming: it's not an ideal situation. I don't see that farming on the scale we can do here will continue to support what it has to support here. That's the dilemma which waits to happen, almost everywhere you have a big house or set of landscape gardens which costs something to keep going."

Patrick Annesley lives in Annesgrove House, near Castletownroche in North Cork. There have been gardens around the house for over 200 years. Much of the work in laying out the gardens as they now are was done by Patrick's grandfather a century ago. The gardens are open to the public from March 30 to September annually.

Jim Ryan

"It all goes back to a GAA background, in Watergrasshill. The pitch was just across the road. My father was always involved. He was a good handballer in his day. My brother, Eamonn, known to all in Watergrasshill as 'The Master,' played with Cork in the All-Ireland football final in 1967. He was involved with the Cork county team for years, as a selector and coach. My late brother, Mick, played minor hurling with Cork, and my two sisters played camogie. I had to be involved!

I played hurling. I was a big youngfella: I was the same height as I am now when I was 14. I used to play full back; there was no need for a goalie: I covered the whole area. I used to play with the junior team at home.

The first soccer international I was at was the best I've been at. Brazil came over here after winning the World Cup. They played an Irish team, Shamrock Rovers disguised as an Irish team, an all-Irish team. The likes of Jennings, Rice and Hamilton from the North and Giles from the South.

It ended up 4-3 in Lansdowne Road. That was my first one up there. I got hooked then and I started going to all the matches in Dublin. My first one away was in '76 when I went to London, the match in which Dave O' Leary won his first cap.

Over time, I met friends and we started travelling together. We made several attempts to retire but we never did. I don't drink and the lads drink very little, so, when we go to matches, we go on a different mission to the other supporters, who have to find the pub. I suppose it's a bit like drink and gambling. I was addicted to both of them, but I got out of them. This is a nicer kind of addiction. When you're drinking it's nice, but you fall down. When you're gambling, if you're unlucky, everything goes in one go. We enjoy one another's company, we have a nice time, we don't have to get pissed.

We plan ahead all the time. I booked for the game against Israel next Easter during the summer, because I feel the closer we get to Easter the harder it would be to get there. The one thing about soccer is you always have to be thinking ahead. The next match after that is the Faroe Islands and I was on the Internet last night trying to figure out how to get there. Someone suggested we go to Aberdeen and get a ferry over. I can't find a ferry yet, but we're getting there. It's all forward planning.

It is a great way to see the world. I had to go to Athens for the Olympics and I had to go through Corfu and I was there for two days. How people do this for two weeks, sit by the swimming pool and playing dead? Beyond me. Last week we were in Basle, in Switzerland. I've been in Baku, Azerbaijan for the hockey European Championships. My nieces are good hockey players, play for Ireland, so I started following them. It's all sports, wherever it leads me. It's an addiction.

But the bottom line is we always come back for the hurling. We were worried before the All-Ireland final in 2004 because we thought the only free date, if there was a replay, would be the night we were flying out to France for the World Cup soccer qualifier. Luckily, we won anyway!

I would never miss a Watergrasshill match. I'd never miss a Cork match either. I was the Chairman of Watergrasshill for three years; it didn't go down well that the chairman would go away to soccer matches! But, at the end of the day, there is only one place to come from: Watergrasshill."

Jim Ryan is a retired Garda, living in Killeens, on the outskirts of Cork city. He travels the globe following the fortunes of Irish sports teams, always coming home whenever Cork or Watergrasshill are playing.

Margaret Griffin

"All hell breaks loose in the spring. Cars on the road and everything. We're putting in more car-parking space next year. We have space for about 200 at the moment, but in the very busy time in the spring, it's always spilling out onto the road. You know, there could be 30 cars on the road! It's sort of nice to have succeeded in a business so far out from town, 'cause it wasn't an ideal position really, starting off. But even though we stayed here, town has moved out, so we're in a better position now than we've ever been.

Everyone says that a business fails in the first three to five years. So, in the first three to five years you're just making sure that you survive and keep your head above water financially. And it was slow to get developed. It was hard. It was tough going. Certainly people wouldn't have had the amount of money that they have now to spend, disposable income. It was a tough time to survive in a business. But again, probably because I did it very small and took it step by step, I didn't have huge repayments.

The master plan probably came once I was in operation for about eight years and I started looking at garden centres in the UK and places, between different conferences and consultants.
If I was starting from a greenfield site, we certainly would do some things different. But at the moment, now, we have a consultant who does a lot of the large garden centres in Ireland and he would say that we've got it right in a lot of the things – maybe by chance, maybe by accident, some of them!

I suppose people are so conditioned now by supermarkets: to get in somewhere doing their business fast and getting back out again then. So when they go to a garden centre they have to have the whole thing: automatic doors, nice walkways, trolleys – you know, the whole efficiency thing, like a supermarket. Then, because we're a destination garden centre really - people travel a long way to us – that's where the restaurant comes in. So you can stay almost the full day if you want, with a family.

I have seen a big change in the last 20 years. What we call 'lifestylers' now – people with very little time and lots of disposable income – they want everything instantly: a pot made up that they can just put into the car and take home; the barbeque, not in a box but, would you be able to make it up for them and sit it on their patio when it's delivered! If somebody decides they want a barbeque, they want it to have a barbeque tonight. It's like that now. 20 years ago very few people would have a barbeque or a patio heater in the garden. In May this year they were just walking out of the place.

Everybody decides very quickly what they want. So you have to have everything instant for people.

Three years ago, when things were really, really booming, garden centres didn't do as well as they should have, not as well as other businesses, because people didn't have time to garden: they were either on holidays or long weekends away or they were jetting away the whole time. I think this year people are spending more time at home because the economy has got a bit quieter. But I think we've built up a good name now and people come out to us anyway. That's nice."

Margaret Griffin runs Griffin's Garden Centre in her native Dripsey, County Cork. After qualifying in horticulture, she trained as a florist in England before returning home to set up her garden centre 20 years ago.

Kathleen Geary

"I left Cobh when I was 19. Wanted to do something different. Just wanted to get away, couldn't wait to get away. The usual. Left home and went over to the bright lights and excitement, to London.

I think it was 1986 I went. It was quiet here, but you know the way you're a bit footloose after you come out of school, and you don't really want to settle down at anything. So, let's try something new and head off! So, I went away and worked in a hotel over there. It was an Irish hotel: the London Tara, owned by Aer Lingus. They did a big recruitment drive over here, because they liked to have Irish staff. They put you up in a hostel, and obviously, they'd give you smaller wages because they were actually housing you. But they gave you free flights, two a year, summer and Christmas, which was fine. Did me!

I enjoyed my time there, but I think as you get older, you get more of a sense of wanting to get back. Well, I did: I wouldn't be a city type of person at all.

You can be anonymous in London, which for some people is fine, but when you come back on holidays, and I have a fairly big family network at home…I missed that. I wouldn't say I was homesick, or I would have come home earlier, but I think one of the main reasons I came was that my father died. When I got home, my mother was living on her own at that stage, so I said, 'I'll try Cobh again.'

I didn't work initially: there wasn't a whole lot there. So I knew I would have to improve my qualifications if I was to get anywhere. My partner was very supportive. He pushed me into doing this. I'll be honest with you: it was very daunting for someone who's out of school for that length of time. But I went back to Cobh Community College, and they've a really good team up there: Máiréad Goode runs the Adult Education programme up there. So we went through, and did a year's course in everything from computers, secretarial, personal development, you know, all that. It gives you that bit of confidence.

For me, support was important. I have a daughter, so I needed someone to pick her up from school if I wasn't going to be there and who'd fall into the breach, as it were, while I tried to improve our status, and it did work. But I couldn't have done it without him. And even today, there are times when I think, 'Thank God I have somebody at home.' Because, obviously, there are times you have to go to Dublin, to London, you have to go here and there, and it's nice to be able to have someone to lean on. Family is very important. And that's one of the reasons I want to live here: it's a good place to raise a family.

I didn't realise how much I missed it until I was away. I was only in England for four years but it was surprising, how much you'd miss the place. And it was London, so the main thing I missed was the sea. I love the sea! I love being by the sea. I missed being able to walk down the street and say, 'Hello' to people, even though they didn't know you. They mightn't really know you, but they still said, 'Hi.' A sense of community really, which you have in Cork in general and in Cobh in particular."

Kathleen Geary is the Chief Executive of Cobh Chamber of Commerce. She began to work there in 1995, on a FÁS scheme, rising gradually through the ranks. She lives on the outskirts of the town with her husband and their daughter, having returned home to Cobh from London in the early '90s.

Kevin Dwyer

"I was born in Cork in 1944. My education started in the Christian Brothers, briefly, and then I was sent to a prep school in Sussex.

When I came home from school in 1962 and started in Sunbeam, I was very much a foreigner in my own land. It took me quite a while to develop friends because I had been brought up in a sort of a different background. My career in Sunbeam gravitated towards the marketing side of things.

In 1970 I got married to Fiona. At the same time I became Advertising Manager for Sunbeam and I managed an advertising budget then that would be equivalent today to about, you know, well over a million Euros. So it was a big spend. We went all over Ireland setting up pretty sophisticated photoshoots. By 1973 recessionary times started hitting. In 1974, I felt that I would not be retiring from the job in the textile industry at the age of 65.

So I found a job in the banking world, in a small bank called the Commercial Banking Company Limited. The bank was taken over by Barclays Bank in 1982. Barclays didn't get it very right in Ireland. In 1986 I was faced with the opportunity or threat of voluntary redundancy, at the age of 42, with two children in secondary school – which was quite scary on reflection. Within a few months, my brother Peter who had his own fashion business said to me - he knew that I was a keen amateur photographer – 'Look Kevin, you set up all of these fashion shoots yourself – why don't you consider photographing my collection?'

So I photographed my brother's collection and this led me to go forward, into commercial photography and eventually, into the skies.

In 1995 I went to New York to the Yacht Club to present my aerial photographs of the Irish coastline to some American yachtsmen who were being invited over to a cruise in 1996. When I was going to the States, I rang Tommy Barker, who worked in the Examiner at the time, and I said, 'Tommy, do you realise I've been invited to the New York Yacht Club?' And he said, 'Wow!' And I said, 'Can I send you in some of the photographs?' And the Examiner did a two-page feature. But the important aspect of all of this was the fact that Cork publisher, Con Collins, saw the feature and he rang me up and said to me, 'Kevin, I'd love to publish a book of your work.'

So in 1996 I created, 'Ireland, Our Island Home: an aerial tour around Ireland's coastline.' The book was published in 1997. And whereas a coffee table book doesn't make it to the best-sellers list, this book did, for the best part of six to eight weeks, which was absolutely astounding.

Looking back over my career, I look around with horror at the pressure that children are under today with the Leaving Certificate and points. I personally feel that I went to the university of life in Sunbeam Wolsley. It was a fantastic place. And I think that having come back from school in England with no knowledge of this place called Ireland, I had this sort of mission in my life to find out about it. I think I've gone out and visualised it through my own eyes, and I've had the great fortune of being able to share with everybody else what I found, through my books."

Kevin Dwyer is the grandson of Billy Dwyer, the "black sheep" of the Dwyer family, who left the family business to set up Sunbeam Wolsley. Kevin's career has taken him from marketing executive to photographer and author. His second book, 'Ireland: the inner island,' was also a bestseller.

Owen O'Callaghan

"There's a guy, Yuri Sedhyk, he still holds a world record, for the hammer. He came over here in 1984 when we were sponsoring the hammer event at the Cork City Sports. And he came over here and he broke the world record. And we were delighted: we brought him out on the town that night.

And he loved his pints. But he'd no money. We fed him.

So, the following year, Quinnsworth decided to sponsor the Sports and they took it from us. We were only sponsoring the hammer, but Quinnsworth took the whole thing, including the hammer, because they knew he was coming. And this time, he was coming to break the record again. But he came over two days in advance…and he came looking for me. He wanted more Guinness. I met him two nights before the Cork City Sports event. I had to meet him both nights. He wouldn't go away, he wanted pints. Pints. He couldn't lift the hammer the day of the event! Quinnsworth, they won't take another event from us, y'know.

I was much happier out on the actual site. To this very day – even though I don't do it any more and I miss it badly – I would be as happy as Lar standing in the middle of a big site and all these machines moving around the place, levelling it off and all that. That's where I'd love to be. But I haven't been there for 15 years now. But that's probably my favourite location: where things are happening. Not inside in a bloody office!

I meet the chairman of the local community association in Mahon once a week. He's in here every Monday morning – unless I'm missing, in which case it's Tuesday morning – just to update each other on everything that's happening. That is vital. The local people will be employed down there. But that's the buzz, that's the good side of it. I'm not saying I'm one of these goody, goody two shoes who goes around running these things, but it just works out well. You get a buzz.

I don't switch off, honestly. Other people I know, they can cut off completely and go away and do things. I couldn't go way and play golf in the middle of the week. I should do that, but I just can't concentrate. That's not good for you. Tomorrow's a Saturday, I've two dogs - my two best friends – and I live in Upper Rochestown, and I'll walk around there with the dogs. I might go for a game of golf – might – on Sunday, with my wife. I can't concentrate on golf. I look forward to Monday morning and getting back into action again. Monday starts off with meetings again, and I enjoy it. What else am I going to do?

I was trying to get a bit interested in sport – more interested in sport - when we had a tragedy. My daughter was killed, and that finished that. I just pulled out of that completely. I'd be very slow now to go to functions or those things now. Basically, when that happens to you, you lose a part of your life. I figure, about 25%. The enjoyment side of life disappears – at my age too – when that happens to you. Terrible. I was always giving out to her for driving a car too fast, y'know. And then, a bloody horse. We had a lot of horses at home, but we sold them all, got rid of them all, and we have a selection of stables and horse walkers at home, all rusting away."

Owen O'Callaghan founded O'Callaghan Properties Limited in 1969. He decided to branch out into property development in the 1980s, building Ireland's first multi-storey car-park outside Dublin in Paul Street, in Cork city centre. Currently, the company is developing the massive Mahon Point project. His daughter, Hazel, died tragically two years ago. He lives on the outskirts of the city with his wife, Sheila.

Noreen Minihan

"Lots of people ask me how teaching has changed. I find the greatest change is that children have got more confidence in themselves. Because of television they are very aware of what's happening. Because of television you have to be very active with them. You have to be kind of a cross between Big Bird and Barney. You've got to keep their attention all the time. In my time everybody was on the same page at the same time in their reader. But now, a child in, we'll say, first class, could be doing the reader from fourth class. And when you have 56 in a class, you'll appreciate the fact that it might be difficult to make sure that every child is going ahead at a good pace!

And they are more forward I suppose. They're noisier than what they used to be. They're very quick to pick up. And they question more now, of course. I find anyway that they're very with it. They're into nature, they're into the universe and they're into all kinds of things like that. And want to know more. They're big into projects and hands-on experience of things. You don't have to tell them as often about something. But, in reality, I suppose, a child is a child, when you come down to it.

Certainly, now, from a teacher's point of view, it wears you out. Because you go in in the morning at ten-past-nine, and OK, you have a break for 10 minutes for lunch, and then when it's lunchtime, you're on duty. The 10-minute break would be a tea break and then at lunchtime you're on duty most times. So, you can't relax for a minute with them. Some people can't understand but mostly I enjoy the children. And I love being with them. And I look forward to going over to them. There's no Monday morning that I mind getting up and going over. It's not so much the challenge as the interaction with the children. And I enjoy, I suppose, feeding them the information and seeing how they respond to it and seeing how they remember it.

They're well-fed and well-clothed and well looked-after as well now; the children I've met anyway! There were hard times in Clon before. Well, I suppose to a certain extent they were. I mean, t'isn't everybody would have meat all the time. Remember, the families were bigger: I mean, I've taught families who had 10, 11, 12…I've taught a family who had 17. I've taught a family with 19. So families were much bigger. And parents were absolutely marvellous. They really were. I know one lady now and they had the family of 12, and they had only two bedrooms until they turned the sitting room into another bedroom. And those children were always immaculate. And she really kept her eye on all the children to make sure that they wouldn't fall behind. When they grew up, they all did well.

And I remember the convent. I remember the nuns used to come down the town. I mean, now, all the heart people tell you 'tis all wrong, but they had dripping – they'd have dripping from doing beef – and they'd bring it round to the houses of big families and needy families with a cake of brown bread so they could fry the bread in the dripping. And t'would be good nourishment. Nowadays they don't think that's such a good thing."

Noreen Minihan, whose family have lived in Clonakilty for generations, was Principal of the infant boys' school for 30 years. As well as being active in the local community, she still works as a substitute teacher.

Deirdre Clune

"My father was always involved in politics. His father before him – my grandfather – Anthony Barry, was Lord Mayor of the city, was involved in the council for many years and was WT Cosgrave's election agent. So, it was always in my father's family. Then, my father worked as my grandfather's election agent and, I suppose, he got the bug.

I was living with it all the time. We were really involved with it. At home, it was always there; politics was just part of it: he was busy, his phone was always ringing and there were people at the door. Election time, you just got busy with whatever had to be done: envelope stuffing or making tea and sandwiches for the workers, the canvassers. I remember as a teenager being called in to distribute leaflets outside polling booths – as you were allowed to do at the time.

I remember my grandfather being Lord Mayor. Vaguely! I would have been very young! My earliest political memory would be of my father being elected to the Corporation, which would have been in '67. Then, in '69, he stood for the Dail and he was elected for the first time. The reason he stood was that he felt that there was no opposition to Fianna Fáil at the time and he felt that someone had to stand up and provide it. He said he was going to give it 10 years – two terms – but circumstances took over…

I remember that election in '69 and I remember Liam Cosgrave forming a Government in 1973. My father was Minister for Transport and Power. I'm sure I could name all the members of that Government for you. I was too young to canvas, but I remember helping my mother with the supplies for the troops. They were exciting times. I suppose: it was what you were reading about in the papers and it was happening in your house; it was in your circle.

When my father retired, really, it was around that time that I started thinking about running for office. It's one thing getting the job and doing it, but it's another thing getting yourself elected, because you need neck for that and an awful lot of energy to get a lot of people to work for you, to commit to you.

I was willing to take a chance on it though. I was approached and I decided it was something I could do. 'Politics?!' most people would say: they'd get a shiver from it. But having lived with it, I knew it and I had confidence that I'd be able to do it and that I'd be able to deal with it in my life, because it does expand into every spare corner that you have. I decided that it was an opportunity and if I didn't throw my hat in the ring, I might always regret it. It wasn't like it was a burning ambition of mine, but once I was elected to the Dáil then in 1997, I loved it.

Politics is so demanding of anybody. It's not a nine-to-five job. Four nights of this week, I have meetings. That doesn't give you a chance to take a walk, go to the cinema, go to the pub for a pint. It is difficult; you're juggling all the time. It's Saturdays, can be Sundays as well. But I like it. Wouldn't have it any other way. That's probably because I grew up with it, saw it at home and knew that that's the way things were. It's not a shock to me, it's not a surprise to me, it's just the way things are. And you do it."

Deirdre Clune is a Fine Gael member of Cork City Council. Her father, Peter Barry, who was at one stage Minister for Foreign Affairs, sat in the Dáil from 1969 to 1992. After the death of Hugh Coveney, Deirdre stood for election and became a member of the Dáil in the 1997 general election. She lost her seat five years later, but hopes to regain it at the next election.

Conor Phelan

"It would have been difficult to get a prescription after 6pm at the time. Some pharmacists could be knocked up and would come down, but there was nobody offering our service: we opened seven days a week until 10 o'clock in the Regional Late Night Pharmacy in Wilton.

It was, initially, costly to open those hours. But within a short period of time, people started using the service. You can go in there every night now, 365 days: we open Christmas Day and everything. Not for the whole day, but 364 days a year we were open every night and we gave a few hours Christmas Day just to continue the service. I think that was appreciated. A lot of people thought we were an all-night pharmacy, but we were only ever open until 10 o'clock.

When we did it, it was a huge risk for us; all our advisors would have advised us against it: they felt that the cost of opening those hours wouldn't be justified, that it was a 35-year lease we were tied into with no way of getting out of it. But at the time, we'd no children. Still, it was a big plunge for us to take. The bank even refused us a loan to do it. Looking back, people say, 'Sure it was obviously going to be successful,' but at the time, there were no late-night pharmacies in Cork, and we thought that it would probably get more business from the hospital than from the late-night side, but in fact, it turned out the opposite. Then regular business followed.

Hindsight is a great thing, to see the opportunity afterwards. At the time, all our advisors, bar my mother, would have said, 'Go away and think about it, you're making a mistake' and we had to say, 'We're going to do it!' Is that the difference between success and not being successful? It can come down to a decision like that. It could equally have failed. Who knows?

I didn't study science for my Leaving Cert. I was leaning towards doing accountancy, which my parents thought might suit me better: I'd have had weekends off! My mother was a chemist as well, and she said, 'You'd be working seven days a week!' But, on the day I was filling in the CAO form, I decided on pharmacy.

I grew up with pharmacy. My mother and two uncles were pharmacists, and my grandfather was a druggist. I worked in a pharmacy from when I was a young kid, stacking shelves and all that. I liked it, and I still like it. I still enjoy working behind the counter.

If you choose the right location and open a pharmacy in the right place, you should be able to make a commercial success out of it, if you put in the hours. It wasn't without a lot of hard work along the way for me. There are pharmacists that haven't succeeded, and back then, there were pharmacies that opened and didn't succeed.

When we sold up, it was mostly for lifestyle reasons. The mobile's stopped ringing every 30 seconds. There's only so many years you can work at that pace for. So it was nice to take a break. Absolutely no regrets. We're not sitting back and doing nothing either. We're getting involved in other businesses, other challenges. But I'd hope never to be in a seven-day business again, open until 10 o'clock at night."

Conor Phelan and his wife, Denise, sold 10 of their chain of 12 pharmacies in 2003. They still retain two outlets, in Carrigaline and Glanmire. Conor set up first in Carrigaline in 1988, before opening the city's first late-night pharmacy near Cork University Hospital in 1992, and going on to establish a chain of outlets around Cork.

John Brogan

"I went across the water and I didn't know whether to go left or right after getting out of Paddington Station, that's the truth. I'd no fare, nothing. I slept in Hyde Park for about two weeks and then I met a Cork fella and he put me up. I got a job in the Cumberland Hotel, where over three or four thousand Corkmen, Irishmen, got a job until they got on their feet. I started on the building then.

I came up then, up, up, up. They made me foreman, then manager. Then I took over SGB scaffolding in Great Britain. The boss said to me, 'John, what are you going to do? The firm is yours to take over: do what you like.' I bought more lorries, more scaffolders and hired all Irishmen. And then, I said, 'These signs have to come down.' They had big signs, for carpenters, bricklayers, scaffolders and so on: 'No Irish.' Then, across the road was a big, big pub, and there was a placard: 'Rooms to Let: No Irish.' And my blood was boiling. 'One day, very soon…' I said. And, when I took over the firm, I'd all the signs taken down. I put up new ones: 'Only Irish need apply.' The police came – Scotland Yard! 'Get the hell out of here,' I said, 'this is private property.'

The working conditions were shocking. Shocking. And for the Irish, it was worse. They used to go to work and they used to sleep in their clothes. There was a lot of them slept in Hyde Park with me when I went over. You couldn't get anything. Only for the Cumberland Hotel, there's a lot of people would have been dead.

I got a flat and then there were people knocking on the door. People'd leave Cork and say, 'What'll I do, Mam?' 'You just knock on Johnny Brogan's door and he'll do the rest.' I never turned no one away. Everyone, I gave them a job or I set them up with work. They were sleeping on the stairs at times: I'd give 'em blankets. God help us, they used to knock at two or three in the morning. I used to hear them knocking and I used to say to myself: 'That's a little Johnny Brogan knocking on the door.' There's many nights I cried.

A lot of kids ran away from Cork, little girls. I sent them back home. I paid their fares and I phoned their mothers or Johnny O'Mahony. Johnny used to write to me, and some people used to phone me: 'Mr Brogan, me daughter's run away.' I'd be waiting at the station for them. Back straight again. Then, some of 'em would get away and you'd never catch 'em. It was very hard. But I dedicated my whole life, because of the poverty I suffered here.

We lived in one room in Cattle Lane. They came from Limerick, Dublin, Waterford. Travellers. All stayed in Cattle Lane, in the tenement houses. We had no electric light, we had no gas. We used go out the country for bits of wood to boil a cup of tea: this is the Gospel truth. We used to go out the country and get bags of chaff and we'd sell it for fourpence a bag. That was a mattress. They were the beds and the pillows. That were our beds in Cork. That did for 12 months until the next harvest and then you'd change your bed. It was poverty and I always cried over it: that's why I helped thousands of people. I never forgot Cork and the poverty."

John Brogan's house in London was home – sometimes only briefly – to hundreds of Corkonians and Irish people who emigrated to England. He left Cork himself in 1943.

Una Murray

"I'm from a place called Rockhill in County Limerick. I moved to Cork in the late '70s. I worked in bars around the city for about 25 years. I was happy with bar work. I loved meeting people. In the meantime, I met a Corkman got married and we had two children. Unfortunately he died 10 years ago. Then I met a man from West Cork, Finbarr McCarthy, and we now have a three year old, Patrick.

I came to live in Mahon in the very early '80s. At that time, there were no houses on the other side of the main road. And even then, all the houses on this side weren't built yet. The place was virtually a building site when I came down here. It didn't take long before it all became built-up. Like all other city suburbs, it has its joys, and its problems.

When my children were young I got involved in the youth club, set up by people who had young kids, hoping that they would have a place to go. A lot of the kids in the youth club when I was involved in it have gone on now to work in Community Development Projects – they're working with the youths themselves.

It was a battle all the same. It's still a battle, even now with the community centre. You have huge problems there with regard to insurance. You get a lot of complaints about, 'We can't do this, you can't do that,' but people don't seem to understand that you have to have insurance. The centre is chock-a-block at the moment with all the different groups.

We got a new manager there a while ago, Denis Corcoran, and he's formed a book club, which is mainly aimed at retired people, or those living alone. They go maybe twice a month and they swap books, tell each other about the books they've read, and recommend books to each other. It's kept going, but you can only do so much. With regard to the choices you have, there's always people that won't be happy. They'll say, 'I want to do this.' But, it's impossible to do everything. Absolutely impossible. Financially and physically: I've a small child, I've a house to run. Between meetings and God knows what, it takes up a huge amount of time.

I used to be chairperson of the Community Association when there was very bad smog here. During the wintertime, when the temperatures were frosty, you literally couldn't see the houses across the road. They were all built with coal fires, open fires: one in the kitchen and one in the front room. We decided that it was time to clean up the air in Mahon. So, we started a campaign to get rid of smog. After a five-year battle, we eventually did get Cork declared a smog-free zone. It's been a massive improvement – not just here, but in other parts of the city as well.

I know there are more council houses here than there are private houses. The main thing is there are a lot of decent, honest people here. I think at times, too much attention is paid to the negative stuff. I always try to be positive, to keep things upbeat, not to be running things down.

The last 10 years have been great for Mahon. A lot of people, including myself, have bought the houses they were living in. Even to drive down the road here, you can see how well-kept the houses are. People got jobs and maintained jobs, sent children to college. It's made a big difference. It has been good for the area."

Mother-of-three Una Murray is a community activist in Mahon. She was born and bred in Rockhill, County Limerick before moving to Cork in the late 1970s. Her husband died 10 years ago, leaving her with two children. She had a third child with her current partner.

Brian O'Donnell

"An old fella used come in here long ago, from Great Universal Stores, and he told me that the ground floor part of a shop took 40% of the takings. The other four floors had 60% between them, and they had to rotate the ground floor display. It was a fairly demoralizing statement for me!

So, I suppose I made it against the odds. Being outrageous helped, I suppose. A bit eccentric, maybe.

I love a joust. Anyone who thinks they can beat me in a verbal joust is fooling themselves. My grandfather, Michael K Barry, was the first chairman of Cork County Council.

He had a marvellous vocabulary. He could put people in their place. You'd have to see me in action: 'tis like a courtroom scene.

I'm well-read. I'd say an awful lot of publicans aren't as well-read as I am. 'Tisn't a load, I'm not particularly proud of it or anything. Anyone can be read. The poorest person can be the best read. 'Tisn't a scholar's thing.

You learn nothing by talking, even though I am now. You learn it by reading or listening. And of course, as Johnson said, some years ago, 'The best conversationalist is the best listener,' and though it doesn't suit me, I have to go with the flow.

I'm probably the poorest publican in Cork, not maybe financially, but for having been 47 years at it! As Jude used to say long ago, 'Money is that which only enables you to enjoy your miseries in comfort.' And, one of the great grand slam players in America said, 'I don't want to be a millionaire, I just want to live like one.'

I studied medicine but never practiced, never got that far at all: I'm only a three-eights doctor. It's funny how all the consultants, the teaching doctors, they were saying to me, 'All medicine is observation.' When you come into a doctor, you have to tell him what's wrong with you, and he has to figure it out, make a diagnosis. Then I came into the bar game, and what did I find? All observation again. So, I suppose it's life all over: observation, diagnosis and making up your mind.

But my big thing in life is to have the musical interest. I'm on two planes: I'm into popular music, and classical music. All types. I could go from Miles Davis to Burt Bacharach to the historic recording of the Mahler Ninth done by Bruno Walter in Vienna in 1938 and I'd be equally at home.

In any pub, I don't care what they play, as long as the music isn't too loud. That people are able to talk to each other: that's the criterion in my book."

Brian O'Donnell took over the Hibernian Bar on Oliver Plunkett Street nearly 50 years ago, after his father died of lung cancer. The 'Hi-B' is one of Cork's landmark pubs, situated on the first floor of a city centre building, and has attracted visitors from around the world. Brian lives overhead.

Áine Hyland

"Education, for me, is my life. It's everything that I care about and everything I work for and with. In my view, education is the tool that can develop, and change, and conserve society in the best possible way. So, for me, the university plays a really central role in any society, but that's particularly true, in my view, in Cork, because Cork is a university city. One of the main employers in Cork is the university. One of the main influences in Cork is the university. It contributes to the economy, it contributes to the culture, to everything that the city is about.

I think the great things, certainly in my lifetime in UCC and particularly during the last five years, are the increasingly close links that the university has forged with the community in Cork. And that goes from Early Childhood Education – the first degree of its type that was ever developed on this island – to a project which I run myself, which I got private money for: 'Bridging the Gap.' We have 40 schools with which we work very closely: we invite them into the university; we go out and see them in the schools; we support them in whatever way we can. That's been a tremendous development.

It's been very successful. Even in terms of the numbers of students. I mean, any one student who comes to us who wouldn't traditionally have come to us, that's a huge success story for that young person and for their family, but numerically, we now have quite a significant number of students in the university who have come through the access programme into the university to do all kinds of courses. It took a while. When the access programme began to develop in the early to mid '90s it took quite a few years to build that relationship with the schools and with the families in those under-represented communities. But since it consolidated in 2000 or thereabouts, the numbers have begun to grow very rapidly.

We would find with particularly the older members of the family – the parents – that UCC would be a no-man's land to them. And indeed, as one said to us recently, the only memories they would have had of UCC would have been of being chased off the grounds for trespassing! Some of the communities would have been fairly suspicious initially, given the historical relationship they had with the university.

Or, I mean, they always saw it as a potential employer for cleaners and for security, for groundspeople, but they didn't see it as an educational place for themselves. That has begun to change, although it's still a bit of an uphill struggle. But of course, UCC wouldn't be unique. That would be true all over the world; that university education was simply not seen as something to which these communities would aspire.

The existence of a university in a city is hugely important in developing economic links. If you talk to people in the IDA they will emphasise the importance of the university and an Institute of Technology in the city, to enable them to bring industry into Cork. Outside of Ireland, the big professions have always been closely linked with universities. That has been their strength because the whole economic environment is always changing. It would be remiss of a university not to keep up with that and support whatever economic needs the community has."

Professor Aine Hyland is Vice-President of University College Cork. Her professional career began as a civil servant in the Department of Education in the 1960s. She trained as a teacher and worked in secondary schools for a time before moving to Third Level, where she taught in Trinity College, Dublin, Carysfort College, and University College, Dublin. She first came to UCC as Professor of Education in 1993.

Donal Kelleher

"I played with Togher Rovers up to about 16 or 17. I broke my leg then so I went out of football.

I went back alright for a bit with Cork Celtic's reserves. But t'wasn't working out for me, you know? So I decided then at 17 years of age to start a schoolboy team up.

We used to play in our own green before we went into the street leagues that time. There was an arch there, so, we used to come up by that arch. We'd the best of gear and we'd march out like t'was Wembley.

And we entered the Togher Street Leagues, which we won all around us. So we had a lot of trophies and everything. When the youngest then came to about 11, we entered into the under-12 league, Cork Schoolboys' League. And where I live is Kilreendowney Avenue and we needed a name for the team, so we took the Kilreen out of that and I used to follow Cork Celtic, so I took the Celtic out of that and founded Kilreen Celtic.

In 1971, our first year, we'd one team under-11, played in the under-12 league. We got to the League and Cup semi-final, but we lost both. But the year after we beat Crofton Celtic in a kind of local derby here in Ballyphehane and won the league.

Then the following year we worked different teams all the way up. After that, we went to under-16 football, then, we went to junior football. We got a few parents involved that time too and they came in and you know, we just worked from there.

We played in Ballyphehane Park: that was the main pitch. Every club in Cork used it: t'was like a home ground for clubs that had no grounds. And t'was like a road that time: the glass on the pitch and everything was unbelievable. Like a road: just bare now down the middle. Bare completely. Hard stones sticking up. If the sun was shining and you were up at the top, you could see the glass shining. But then eventually clubs were getting their own grounds and at the moment only ourselves and Casement use the pitch, which has been done up and everything, so it's better!

The coaching has changed as well. Like, that time you'd just exercise and take a few free kicks. There was no such thing as the coaching that is there now. We'd just run up hills and down again.

We're going to build new dressing rooms now. The players need that; they need to go into a good, clean dressing room after being out, maybe have a shower. There's the heating as well. Now, they're coming in cold and there's probably water on the ground. But these new dressing rooms, they'll benefit the players. They'll have somewhere to go to put their clothes away tidy. Their clothes will be clean and dry going out the door. Even for training as well. And everybody in the community, now, has started to get involved to get the money for the dressing rooms.

I'm 51 years of age now and I'm happy with it. Maybe I'll retire sometime… well not from all of it. You couldn't, like, you know what I mean? You'd be saying you would, but you couldn't, you'd miss it. Even when the season is off, the two months when the season is gone, July and August, you'd be restless…you'd be saying, 'Christ, what am I going to do?' I love it."

In 1971, Donal Kelleher founded Kilreen Celtic, which is now one of the city's biggest soccer clubs. He is the Secretary of the Cork Schoolboys' League and a member of the Schoolboys' Football Association of Ireland executive.

Tony O'Dwyer

"Back in the early '80s, on the job front, especially around Cork, there wasn't a whole lot happening: a lot of industries were closing down. What I had been doing, I knew I didn't want to do for the rest of my life; I wanted to do something different with a bit more of a challenge.

I had served my time as a steel fabricator, and I got all my qualifications, but it wasn't something that I wanted to do. I probably could have made a lot of money had I stayed with it, but that wasn't what I wanted to do. It's not that I have anything against making money – I haven't – it's just that I'd have been in a job that I didn't want to do for the next 20 or 30 years.

I suppose what appealed to me was the whole change of scene. In Ireland, you didn't have a whole lot of amenities like this. OK, you had Dublin Zoo but it's so far away that you might have got there about once or twice a year; you certainly wouldn't have gone there on a regular basis. To have some place like Fota on your doorstep was so exciting.

At the time, the Cork Examiner and the Evening Echo would have had a lot of updates on how the Park was developing. At that stage, it was just getting the infrastructure in place and there would have been headlines about cheetahs arriving at Fota,

giraffes arriving at Fota. And as someone down here, down south, it was something completely new; I just saw it as an opportunity. I thought, if I could get in here on this, it could be something that I would enjoy. Now, I've always wanted to work outdoors and even in my previous jobs I would have been outdoors an awful lot, so the idea really appealed to me.

The whole thing sounds a bit corny, I know: being out with nature and things like that. But when I came we had 10 new animal houses, so you would be digging holes for fences, and it was very much a hands-on job, which actually really appealed to me. You were getting stuck in and you were getting dirty, you would finish at the end of the day, tired but satisfied.

Summer obviously is a fantastic time because you've the weather; the winter can be a little bit harder because the weather can be cold and wet but the great thing is to be actually working here in the wildlife park and see the different things unfolding. Spring to summer to autumn to winter and to see the leaves changing colour, falling and then to see young animals being born in the spring…again, it probably sounds a little bit corny but to be right in the middle of that and to see nature happening? It's a great privilege to see it.

I often think a lot of people around the Cork and the Munster area don't realise what they have on their doorstep: it's a fantastic amenity. It's the only wildlife park in Ireland; if people wanted to see the equivalent of what we have here, they would have to go to England and even further afield to see it and yet we have it right here on our doorstep."

Tony O'Dwyer is Park Operations Manager in Fota Wildlife Park, near Cobh in East Cork. He went there initially to do some seasonal work after the park opened and rose through the ranks to become Head Warden before taking up his current position.

Jim Hegarty

"It all started back in 1967. I was looking for a summer job and I saw this ad in the paper: Lorry Helper wanted, apply box number. I got my summer job.

Went back to school, did my Leaving Cert and dropped into the brewery and said if there were any jobs going, they might keep me in mind. To cut a long story short, I ended up back on the same mineral lorry with the same driver. The mineral company at that time was a subsidiary of Murphy's, the West Cork Bottling Company.

The West Cork Bottling Company had a section for wines and spirits. I was put in charge of the wine and spirit store. That lasted until Heineken came along in 1983. I ended up going out on the road as a sales rep for Heineken.

If the current management and employees could walk into the brewery as it was in 1968, they would be stuck for words. It was totally different to what it is now. There was just one little office block. The kegs, when they came down the production line, there'd be just one or two rows of them stacked up, maybe four or five high and that row would probably do us for a week or two. And when you think of it now, there are literally thousands of kegs going out the brewery gate every day. The beer was delivered by horses and drays around town - they were still there when I started in '68 and they were still one or two of them there up to about the mid-70s. Heineken came in and since then, the brewery has been totally transformed. The whole site has been totally changed. Total modernisation is about the only description I can use for it.

If you go back 20 years, in practically every town and village in the country - not to mind the city,- there were numerous pubs up and down every street. You could go through the suburbs of Cork and there was probably a pub every 10 or 12 doors. Nearly all of them were family-run pubs. Maybe most of them were more interested in the company and knowing all the locals, their neighbours. They made good money and worked hard, but as time went on, the structure of towns and cities changed and, even in Cork today, there are some small pubs closing down for good. There's many reasons for all this -and it's not necessarily that business is poor. Sometimes depending on where they're located they're worth more as development sites. What has been happening with family pubs is that, as the children grew up, they weren't interested in taking over the pub. The parents discovered then that they were in the pub on their own and they would gladly settle for a big sum of money.

I met my wife down in Crosshaven, in the old Legion Hall down there. It was all made of old timber and there was a stove in the middle of the hall for warmth during the winter.

Back in those days, a lot of people holidayed locally. These days, we're all off to the airport, going to God knows where. In those days, many people rented some place down in the likes of Youghal, Crosshaven or Courtmacsherry. Day after day, you were swimming, fishing, messing around in the rock pools, down to the merries that night, with maybe a half-crown in your pocket and you kept sixpence for a bag of chips on the way home. It was a lovely, laid-back holiday for us, which we thoroughly enjoyed. They were simple holidays, but very enjoyable. There was always good company, good craic, good banter. And, it worked out well for me as well: I met my best friend ever down there."

Jim Hegarty is a sales representative for Heineken Ireland Limited, who took over Murphy's Brewery in the early 1980s.

Jim, from Ballinlough, is brother of international opera star Mary and a stalwart of Na Piarsaigh Hurling Club.

Emelie Fitzgibbon

"I was working in the English department of the University at the time, I was directing with the Cork Theatre Company and, at a certain point, they asked me would I set up an educational theatre wing. That brought two great interests of mine together: education and professional theatre. I tried it for six months and I'm still here 20 years later! I'm still doing the same thing, except it's grown to a vast extent.

We were set up under what was called the 'Team Work' scheme: it was one of those FÁS schemes set up in the mid-80s because unemployment was so high, when there were an awful lot of wonderful people on the dole. We set it up as a pilot project for six months to see if there was a market for the work. And after six months we got a six-month extension, and then, after that, we got another six-month extension, and we kept clawing at work like that until eventually we separated from the Cork Theatre Company and we got a grant from the Arts Council.

I always remember the sheer joy of getting the first £5,000. When you think of it now you wouldn't do much on £5,000, but it was good and it was so exciting. We also did a piece around that time in the Cork 800 – we did the first performance in the Cork 800, which was about young people growing up in the Northside of Cork city in 1970 – and that got us a lot of attention because production standards were very high; that's a thing that we've always tried to do: to get the highest possible production standards that we can.

While it was very much hand to mouth for the first two and a half to three years, there were always very good people involved. The other person who set up the company with me was Laura Magahy – she's better known now for Temple Bar Properties – and she had a real handle on the finances.

We've grown then over the years: we now do about four major school tours a year; we have two established attached youth theatre companies; we have a very wide-ranging outreach programme; and we also do quite a lot of work abroad. We commission a lot of work, some of which is being produced in the States at the moment, which is great.

In these 20 years, I think Cork has changed a lot, in terms of theatre. I think we are at the beginning of having a significant community of theatres and practitioners in Cork; the city is now tending to keep people and people are coming back to work in the city; whereas, when I started, within the first two years, I'd say half of the original group had gone to Dublin.

I think the quality of the work is very good here in general. But I think we badly need a 250-seater theatre here in Cork for medium scale and experimental professional work, because we go between the 650 of 'The Everyman' and the 100 at 'The Granary.' 'The Granary' is available to students most of the time anyway – and it's a lovely experimental space – but it's not totally available to the community theatre here. That would be a wish not specifically for our work, because we tend to be in schools most of the time anyway, but I just feel the need for some of the good companies. Those venues are just slightly too big or not the style of theatre that they work with, so it would be lovely to see some of them in another venue."

Emelie Fitzgibbon founded and is now Artistic Director of Graffiti Educational Theatres Company. She has served on the boards of Cork Theatre Company, Everyman Palace Theatre, National Association for Youth Drama and Asylum Theatre Company. Her educational theatre productions, mostly for Graffiti but also for Replay and Very Special Arts, have been seen not only in Ireland but also in the UK.

Domino

"I had to come up with a concept that was strong enough to bring my own crowd into Blackpool and that's how I came up with the name, 'Afro Bar.' Something totally different, but I would be able to bring in my own crowd, because they would know what to expect. I started to give the bar an African theme. Because, obviously, it's not just for Cork people only or African people only; it's just a normal bar with an African theme. I brought in African music, obviously, African beer, a few plants, that sort of thing.

That's how the Afro Bar started. Now, we have a lot of regular people from around Blackpool, who didn't come into this bar before, but are coming in now, because they like it. A lot of Irish people like the special beers that we have and they come in for that. Then a lot of coloured people come for the music. They play pool together; they mix very well together.

We sell champagne: the guys who come, they come in a group and they wear the nice clothes and everything, they come with some girls and they want to be extravagant and they buy some champagne. It brings something exclusive to the place, makes the place look good. You don't get many places in Cork where people drink champagne; before, in Blackpool, you wouldn't have sold much champagne! It's kind of classy here: the locals try to look good too, of course!

You have a lot of variety in Cork people. A few people are, like, not open-minded to a lot of things. Then, you have a few people who like to be involved in the kind of thing that we do. And then, you have a few people who don't even know what's going on, because they're not in the scene at all. It's difficult to say, 'Cork people are like this,' or, 'Cork people are like that.' You can't put them all in the same ship. For such a small place, it has a big night scene, which is good. In general, Cork people, they're nice and friendly. There's a good buzz in town. There's not much organised nights or club nights, but the amount of venues and places to go, it's amazing.

I do see that most of my customers, the people I cater for, are stopped in most places. I wouldn't be stopped myself, because, even though I'm coloured, people look at me a little bit differently, maybe because of the way I look or the way I speak or the way I walk, I dunno, so I don't feel any racism personally. But I do see it around. I do see it when I drive my car around and people look, as if to say, 'How can he drive a car like that?'

Cork's very new to this scene, though: five or 10 years ago, you had no coloured people here, so, I suppose, it's a normal reaction. Every country would have that when they get foreign people in, of any colour. You do see a lot of racism, but, then again, a lot of people are open-minded as well, and they want to hang out with coloured people!

But I think, maybe if a girl came home with a coloured guy and said, 'I'm going out with this guy,' I don't think a lot of parents would be happy with that. So, there's some way to go. In a country like Holland, if you come home with a coloured boyfriend, they don't see a difference, but that's because, for the last 200 years, they've had colonies. So, before Ireland is going to be at the same level, that's going to take at least 10 years, maybe more."

Originally from Holland, Domino manages the Afro Bar, on Thomas Davis Street in Blackpool. A qualified graphic designer, he works in information technology by day. After arriving in Cork several years ago, he began running R'nB and Salsa club nights around the city centre.

Jerry Connolly

"I think, when I was six or seven, there was a drag in Whitechurch, I was there with my father, Donal O'Mahony and Gary O'Sullivan. I was hooked on it after that then.

The routine is you get up in the morning and between seven and eight you're gone with your dogs for an hour, hour and a half. Roadwork. If you're working at seven, you've to be up at six. Doesn't matter if it's a cold winter morning, you still have to train them, walk 'em. They're on the best of grub: when you get back it's eggs and Weetabix, Vitamin C, Vitamin E. You walk 'em again at six, seven o'clock, another five, six miles. Give 'em pasta, chicken, all different protein stuff.

You'd be running probably two, three times a week. Pups would go Tuesday and Saturday, senior dogs Wednesday and Sunday. It starts on the first Sunday of March until the last week in September, the All-Ireland.

In a draghunt, you go out and you have four quarters. You dip a cloth in aniseed oil and paraffin oil and you go that way, I go this way – we divide the track out – and we meet back in the finishing field. You leave the dogs out and the first dog that goes over the course and comes back over the line wins.

Mostly, there'd be 40, 50 dogs in a senior draghunt, 20 or 30 in senior maidens and pups usually about 20. In the big drags then – the All-Ireland, the Donal O'Mahony, internationals – you could have up to 70, 80-odd competing. The course'd be about eight or 10 miles. The best dog home on the day. If you win, you win, and if you don't, you don't. You might have to spend one day, two days looking for your dog! But they're the joys of it. Your dog is your pride and joy like.

They're harrier dogs. To buy one in England now you'd be talking three, four hundred, a thousand sterling. And there's no guarantee when they do come that they'll run because there's no electric fencing in England: it's only all sheep wire. Here, you're better off breeding your own pups: they'll know about the wire and getting a kick from a cow.

You have to breed your own, to get hardy breeding. It's no good breeding a fast dog when he won't go through an electric fence. You must have the hardy breeding in a dog. The old hunting dogs would run through anything for you. But the dogs around now, they're all English breeding, they won't do it for ya. I've one dog now, if he was walking along and the lead tripped off his leg, he'd jump up in the air: he'd think he's after getting a belt of wire!

If I won a drag tomorrow, a puppy drag, I'd get €20: wouldn't pay for his breakfast in the morning. A big drag then you might win one or two hundred, but sure when you win then, you buy a drink and buy your friends a drink, sure there's nothing there. It's a madman's sport to be involved in: it's time-consuming like.

I've four kids at home and they're out in the country Tuesday, Wednesday, Saturday and Sunday. It's a great way of keeping your kids out of harm's way, getting 'em a dog. As long as you've a good dog, you might get a place in the first six, win a fiver, whatever. Give the kids the envelope then and they're happy out."

Jerry Connolly lives in Farranree with his family. He is acknowledged as one of the foremost drag hunting trainers in Ireland and has won most of the major events in his sport. He has a long association with the Evening Echo, having delivered the newspaper daily since he was a boy, and still delivers to many homes all over the city.

Maurice Walsh

"My first year, we went to Ballinlough in the city, because that's where the County Championships were on. There was a huge crowd there. And we had six boys entered. The first three guys went in and got stopped in the first round: I knew nothing about boxing. I got 'em into shape alright, but that was about it. The last boxer in the ring was a kid named Brendan Roche. He trains horses for the Arabs now.

So, I turned around to John Hartnett after the first round, and I was delighted to get past the first round! But then Brendan was going out for the second round, and his jaw was sticking way out. And I said, 'John, his jaw's broke or something.' And Brendan looked over at me, came back to the corner and said, 'Maurice, what the hell did you do to me? You put my mouthguard in upside down!' That's how inexperienced I was.

But I went to school after that. I studied under the Cubans for three years and Nicolas Cruz, up in Dublin. And then I got my licence and became coach here and with the international team after a time.

This was the old school in Shanagarry before. There used to be a stage up there where the weights are. My wife went to school here. I was coaching football and hurling up in Russell Rovers, just behind us here. This was all busted up: all the windows were broken, rats were in here, rotting wooden floor. Very bad.

So anyway, Noel O'Brien and our secretary, John Hartnett – he was the brains behind the whole operation – they said they'd revive the boxing club. It was in Cloyne: Father Finn had it, but it was out of operation for 20 years. Noel and John boxed for St Colman's themselves.

They brought six kids in. Billy, my son, was only nine at the time, and he would be the oldest, the others were seven and eight year-old kids. It started to get more kids, maybe 10 or so. But the guy who was supposed to be with the kids, he was a contractor, and he didn't always have the time to be there. So sometimes, I'd hear them screeching, and nobody was in here. So I came in and did exercises after I was finished training the Rovers.

One thing lead to another, and they asked me to take the team over. I said no, because I didn't know much about boxing. Then I saw that the thing was going to fall through, so I hopped in.

Boxing keeps guys on the straight and narrow. We'd one young fella who came in. He was getting in trouble. He had nice parents, but was hanging around with the wrong crowd, and he thought he was a big guy. And it wasn't long, about two weeks, before he found out he wasn't as good as us. And the kid went on to be a good fella afterwards.

The rules here are strict. You have to be on time: if you're late twice, you're suspended for a week. There's no drinking for the younger fellas. The senior guys, for three months before fights, they can't drink. And they all abide by the rules. We've never had any fellas in trouble: it's dope-free around here. None of 'em ever got in any trouble."

Irish-American Maurice Walsh ran the Goalpost Bar in Shanagarry for 29 years before retiring in 2000. Previously, he earned a living playing professional American Football in the Atlantic Coast League in the USA. He also coached highly successful teams in baseball and basketball. Love brought him to East Cork where he helped revive the St Colman's Boxing Club. The club won over 30 All-Irelands between 1985 and 2002.

Tara Byrne

"There are lots of different aspects to what we do, but it's easiest to look at it as two parts really.

One is the physical facility of the factory: the building, the spaces and the equipment in there. That's run like a studio complex. What that means is, we offer working spaces for sculptors, so they come and they rent it for a day, a week, or a year, which is the maximum.

The other half – number two if you like, or the second set of things that we do – is put on events. We have lots of discussions, we organise lectures and we commission both Irish and International artists, so we are always trying to show good work, lead by example and generate discussion

If you were to ask who were the three premier, most famous Irish sculptors of the past 20 years, I'd probably name three Cork sculptors.

Vivienne Roche is internationally known and she's certainly nationally known. Maud Cotter is certainly nationally and internationally known. Eilish O'Connell as well: all people who actually founded the Sculpture Factory. I think that's quite remarkable. Maybe there was something in the air when they studied at the Crawford: they obviously had a good teacher; they really made their mark on the Irish arts scene. Maybe there has been a kind of hiatus since then, but I think that's going to change in the next few years: there will be a couple of very prominent Cork people.

Visual arts is probably considered the most elite of all art forms because it doesn't have many watered down versions. For example, with writing, there are so many different types: children's writing, entertaining writing, literary writing. But visual arts is just visual arts, so, I think people see it as being elitist. It depends on how you look at it: it isn't at all unless it's you, yourself, who decides it's elitist, because you don't feel comfortable with it; it's nothing to do with the thing at all: it's to do with your comfort with it and your level of knowledge about it.

With somewhere like the Glucksman Gallery in UCC, or the Crawford, a big part of their remit is to serve the population and one way of serving the population is trying to make the work as accessible as possible. So, what they are trying to do is make it accessible but not dumb it down. For us, it's not quite the same, because we are not a public institution that is there to serve all the citizens of Cork: we are really there to serve the artist. We are very happy in various small ways to work with the community and we give tours all the time, but we are not out there to try to put work in the public domain that people find accessible.

Ultimately, we want to put work in the public domain that people will find challenging, I suppose. One thing we do is always try to be an advocate for sculpture and visual art, so I suppose in that sense, the more you talk about something, or the more coverage it gets in the paper, or the more it is seen around, the more they get used to it, the less scary it is and therefore the less elitist it appears. So, in that sense we would be very interested in making it less elitist: it's not about making the artist less elitist, it's about how you actually present it. But, if you change the art or if you pick work because you think it's going to be more accessible, then I think that's the road to disaster."

Dubliner Tara Byrne's career in the visual arts has taken her from the National Gallery of Ireland, to the Hugh Lane Municipal Gallery in Dublin, to the Irish Museum of Modern Art, to the National College of Art and Design, to the Arts Council, to the National Sculpture Factory on Albert Road in Cork, where she succeeded Mary McCarthy as director in December 2002.

Joe O'Connor

"In 1961, Cork had two flights a day to London. One in the morning and one in the evening. That was it. We were all great card players! But they were different times: people had loads of time to talk to each other. Back in those days, if you saw 200 or 300 people a day, that was a lot.

There was just a very small terminal. Three or four check-in desks. A couple of little small car-hire desks. Very small shops. A very small restaurant. And the airport was only open from nine in the morning until nine at night. In fact, it used to close on a Saturday at six o'clock. Sundays, it used only open from 11 until six at one stage. It was a very quiet place.

Up to last year, a good few of the staff that started on opening day were still here. They were part of a pioneering group, from when an airport was a kind of glamorous thing. And it was a big challenge as well. There was a lot of pressure: it wouldn't have been doing well for many years. So, there was a good spirit, a very good spirit. Thankfully, it has passed on.

We had a few big things here. The Tuskar Rock disaster of 1968: it was very, very sad, 61 people lost their lives. An awful lot of the people were locals. The airport was inundated with people coming out, enquiring, and we didn't know: it took a long time for them to find the wreckage, even. So, it was very, very traumatic. I remember that distinctly.

There was the Air India crash of 1985 where 331 people were killed, that was also in the pre-counselling days: you just got on with it. But we have a brilliant staff here. The tradition is still there: when the chips are down, the staff will always rise to the occasion, no matter how difficult. Over the years, we've had many, many incidents – not as large as those – incidents at sea in particular. You'd get the RAF, or the Royal Navy quite often, or our own rescue services, bringing in someone off a ship in a helicopter running low on fuel.

It's not just like any ordinary job. We're lucky all of us – myself included – to be working in an airport, because there's always something going on: there's variety; there's action; you see humankind in all its emotions; you see sad and happy occasions.

Observing young people going abroad was very sad, years ago, because it was felt that they were gone. But we've a much better economy now; they're going off by choice, for the adventure and the experience. They know they can come back if they want to and that there are jobs available. But even up to 10 years ago, work was scarce and they were always being exported with little prospect of coming back. That's gone now and 'tis great; I hope that it continues.

From a business point of view, it's gone liberal and it's gone competitive and the punter is benefiting from it. It was a very, very regulated, rule-ridden business up to a number of years ago. Now, people are travelling all year round. It's a totally different ball game now, from 1961, from a work point of view. Everyone is very, very busy, very stretched. You're talking about an average of 7,000 people a day going through the airport now. There's a huge change: people are taking winter breaks and they're taking city breaks and they're going off to shows or whatever; they're travelling here, there and everywhere."

Joe O'Connor, from Blarney, is manager of Cork International Airport. He has been with Aer Rianta for 36 years. He began his career in 1966, with the Department of Transport and Power at Cork Airport. Joe is married to Norrie and they have two daughters, Joe Anne and Mary and a son, Michael. His big interests are popular jazz and fishing.

Bernard Martin

"I lived in a place called Shandon Place on the top right hand side of Shandon Street, Number 1, and directly opposite, there was a little archway that led to a warren of houses leading onto 36 or 38 steps, hence the name, Step Lane.

The soccer games usually started when the streets were empty, where one goal was Church Street and the other goal was John Philpott-Curran Street at the top right hand side. The games were nothing short of a war zone where rules went out the window and the only things that were kept in order were the voices; the voices had to be kept down for some particular reason. On one particular evening, this gentleman, who I believe came back from Dagenham, came out with two ladies and they both watched for a short time. While watching, one of the ladies was struck by the ball into the face and the mood of the three spectators changed instantly. But that didn't stop the lads: the match just carried on as if nothing had happened. When we would reach the end of our soccer match, anything up to an hour and a half later, we would then repair to Healy's; it was a little bit like the aftermath of a rugby match: despite what was done in the game, friendships were cemented immediately after the game and all the bad things that happened during the game were usually forgotten about.

I developed a deep interest in classical music because people would come out of the bars at night and they would spend time finishing in groups what they would have started earlier on.

A lot of people who wouldn't have the courage to sing due to shyness or whatever, they would sing then, because their shyness would be somewhat hidden in the darkness of the evening; and the amount of attention that these people would get would be nothing short of amazing. Some of these guys had a wealth of knowledge of the names which would enthral us on radio.

On Step Lane lived a man named Jimmy O'Driscoll, who had a wide selection of opera records. It was in his house that I first heard Beniamino Gigli singing 'Your Tiny Hand' from 'La Boheme.' I was enthralled. Then, there was a man called Dick Coffey, who had a great bass baritone voice and would sing 'Old Man River' at the drop of a hat.

In the very early '60s, Gigli came to Cork and he gave a recital in the Savoy. As I recall, the cost was prohibitive. But we actually did hear Gigli sing, not inside, but on the outside, because at the back of the Savoy, if you put your ear close enough to the wall, you could hear the high notes of whatever Gigli was singing inside there. 'O Solo Mio,' is what I recall him singing. I only heard bits and pieces and you would have cried at the encore and the hand clapping inside because you couldn't hear the voice above it!

My roots are in Shandon Street. I was the youngest in my family but I wasn't the last to leave: two older brothers left sometime later. I lived close by for a number of years and then I moved to a suburban area where I now reside. But I am very much a Northside man. I believe the term is 'Norrie.' I never heard of it until about 10 or 12 years ago, when this fella said to me, 'You're a Norrie so.' And I said, 'What the hell is a Norrie?' But now it's quite plain to me that I'm a Norrie and proud of it."

Bernard Martin grew up on Shandon Street in the 1950s and has been involved in weight training and bodybuilding for many years. Along with his brother, George, he founded the Martin PT Club, in the shadow of Shandon, about 50 years ago. He was one of the first Irishmen to gain the IFPC physical education qualification in Leicester in the 1960s and is currently involved with Fitton Street gym, which houses the trophies of many champion body-builders.

Aidan Ridgeway

"My grandfather's father died in India and his mother came back to Fermoy with two sons. He was mad about the railway and he was always up on the platform, watching the trains. And the stationmaster gave him a job. He went in as a boy. Then, he came back into Cork and he eventually became a train driver. This was way back in 1868. He retired in 1918 after 50 years: he drove trains all over Ireland. He was John.

My father then, Paddy, went into the railway in 1919 as a cleaner – this was in the steam days. He eventually became a driver, he became a foreman then and he retired in 1969 after another 50 years. I went in in 1943 – the war was on – as a cleaner, as the steam was still there at the time. The diesels came then in 1957 and I became redundant! I went up into the platform as a depot person and I did all kinds of jobs. Eventually, I went back to my own locomotive department in 1962, as a train driver. The diesels were there then, and I was appointed an inspector in 1977. I retired in 1992 after 49 years.

My son now, Aidan Junior, is the fourth generation of Ridgeway train drivers.

In 1943, it was hard to get jobs, but we went in as cleaners. t'was rough at the time actually. The engines were bad, the coal was bad. You went in and you got a scraper, a long piece of tin, and the engines would come in after being out working for a week.

They'd be all mud and dirt and we'd have to clean them. We'd scrape the mud off them and we'd use paraffin oil then too.

I was appointed a fireman on the first of July, 1946, in Mallow. My first job was a freight train to Tralee, from Mallow. 60 miles. It took us 12 hours to go to Killarney and that was only 40 miles. The following day, coming back, it took us 16 hours from Tralee to Mallow. The fire would get dirty back at that time and you'd have to stop and clean it, build it up again. Ten times I cleaned the fire, between Tralee and Mallow. So, t'was rough.

'Tis a great job now though. They have a five-day week now. They did a deal with the company and they have good money. Some weeks now, his days off would be Saturday and Sunday of one week and Monday and Tuesday off the next week, so he'd be off from Thursday to Wednesday. They work a bit longer hours, but 'tis worth it, really. I suppose they have irregular hours, as our jobs always covered 24 hours: even though you'd only have passenger trains running until 12 o'clock at night, you'd have freight trains running all night long. You could be going in at two or three in the morning, but that's the way it goes.

As an inspector, I did the foreman's job on a Sunday, from three to 11. Aidan, when he was a small fella, used to come down with me. He'd stay below with me all day, and we'd go up and down to Cobh on the engines. That's what he wanted, to become a driver. So, he's happy now and that's it. He's flying now, he's up and down to Dublin. He loves it.

I'm very proud that he's carrying on the tradition. And he's thrilled too, to be honest. It's unique, probably something that will never happen again."

Aidan Ridgeway Senior was the third generation of Ridgeways to drive trains. His only son, Aidan Junior, has ensured that the tradition progessed one generation further.

Anne Carroll

"I was born in Barrack Street. My father built St Anne's on Fort Street, opposite the Cathedral. He had a factory across the road, making sweets – Joyce's. He made sweets there for a good few years and then he bought a place down on Drinan Street, off Sullivan's Quay and he moved the factory down there.

I can remember now, Step Lane: there were tenements on the side as you went down Step Lane. My husband was born on Barrack Street, at number 51. His parents were from Macroom and they had this little shop called 'The Dairy.' There was one from Ballingeary and one from Dunmanway. Then there were shops: they went right out onto the road. There was a vegetable one, a shoemaker and there was one further down: a sweetshop. Then, where Read's Court is now, that was a coal yard and turf yard.

Down on the left-hand side then, down by the flower shop as you go down, there was a pawnbroker's there and there was also one up on the corner of Vicar Street. That was how they used to make ends meet.

Fort Street was all tenements. When we were living in St Anne's, across the road was all tenements: three, four-storey tenements. They were very poor in the tenements. Every Sunday, they'd wait until you were after your dinner and they'd come over then for whatever's left. I can remember that now as a child. They were desperately poor: really, really badly off.

They were very hard times. It wouldn't be Barrack Street so much as the lanes off. Forbes Street was one of the ones I could remember the most. But even the houses there along Fort Street – the little red-bricked ones – are pretty small and I know families have 10 and 12 reared inside in those. All they had was one room downstairs and a little yard. I don't know how they reared them. There was one in particular now – the girls are still around, grandmothers themselves now – and they'd all come out, you'd think they had maids behind them: they were immaculate. Their mother used knit all their socks and their sweaters and everything for them.

The Barrack Street Band was famous. Every Sunday morning, you'd go out and listen to the band. As far as I can remember, it used to be around 11 o'clock. They'd go down Barrack Street: they'd never go up, always down. I used to love listening to the band. There was an air-raid shelter in Tower Street: it was up against the barrack wall, along there. It never got used though.

I met my husband through my brother: they were in the scouts together - first the cubs, then the scouts. I was only 16! He asked my father could he take me to the pictures and I'll always remember going out in a hat and gloves: you wouldn't be left outside the door without your hat and gloves.

I was 23 when we got married: 1953. I never heard anyone say a bad word against my husband, even up to today. He was very charitable to people who were very badly off. He wasn't very religious, but he was what I would call a true Christian. He died suddenly. He was only 48.

I wasn't qualified for anything myself. They usen't believe that girls should be qualified for everything: they'd get married and then the husbands would look after them. We never even questioned it: you wouldn't at that time. We were just dressed and fed and whatever.

It's a lifetime, isn't it? Where does time go? Unbelievable, isn't it?"

Anne Carroll was born near Barrack Street. In 1953, she married the pharmacist Gerald Carroll, who died suddenly of a heart attack at the age of 48. She now lives in Douglas.

Sister Rosario

"I was enclosed, so I didn't know much about what was happening on the outside until the 1960s, after Vatican II. Up to then, I knew that there was a lot of poverty and a lot of children needing breakfast. Some still do, mind, but more of them at that time.

They were hard times. Around the locality here, there were a lot of tenement houses. I used to visit an old lady in Evergreen Street when she was sick. She told me they just had a tiny little room: there was just the kitchen where we were sitting: everything was in the kitchen. And a ladder going up to the attic. I think she told me that there were 10 of them reared there.

Things have changed for the better. People are able to afford things now that they weren't able to afford. There was a great tradition of poor people coming up to 'the back door': it's a window off the kitchen. We had loads of people every morning for breakfast and back again at dinnertime to take away food. We built a little house for them so they wouldn't be having their mug of tea in the rain.

For 12 years I taught in the primary school. It was mainly infants I taught. Then I was asked to go to college to do a music degree, so I taught mainly musicianship and choirs in secondary school. I taught many other things as well, especially religion: I always had a religion class. I had to retire at 65: I had to retire officially. The education authority said you can go now and thank you. But you keep on doing a bit, lots of things to be done about the place. We're retired from teaching, not from work.

We became unenclosed after Vatican II. That is what our founder would've wanted: she was never enclosed. She went around visiting the poor and the sick in their homes. Times have changed. Some people thought if you wanted to be a nun you had to be enclosed. Some people didn't like the look of our sisters walking the streets. Some of them called them the walking nuns and even the galloping nuns. But being unenclosed was exactly what Nano Nagle wanted.

It was great when we became unenclosed, to go and do your own messages. To get out whenever you wanted, post your own letters…things like that were great. I don't go out in the city just for the sake of walking or going there: I go when I want something. Don't talk to me about the mobile phones out there! Sometimes I turn around thinking they are speaking to me, but, of course, they are on a phone.

The noise at night can be terrible and it's not from the Douglas Street pubs across the road, it's the other people coming home from town. They seem to come up down Barrack Street and pass our way. You'd swear it was in the middle of the day, even though it's three or four in the morning, shouting and talking as if it was the afternoon. I feel sad for them, because, how are they going to get up the next day? How are they going to get up at all? They must have to keep a job sometime. If I was there I would shut all the nightclubs at 11 o'clock anyway."

From Drogheda originally, Sister Rosario is a nun at the South Presentation Convent on Douglas Street. She was professed on the seventh of September 1940. She is also an authority on Nano Nagle.

Colm O'Herlihy

"I regard adult education in a prison as covering everything that you need to function as an adult in society. If that means knowing how to cook, knowing how to rent a house, knowing how to be a proper tenant, knowing how to access health services, social welfare services, and so on and so forth, that's an education service.

So, we concentrate, obviously, on basic education. We have three home economics teachers who would cover such subjects as cookery, child care, nutrition, sexually transmitted diseases and other such matters pertaining to health that adults should be aware of. And then we have the conventional subjects: wood-work, computers, English, maths, history, art, physical education.

This is an excellent environment if you wish to educate yourself, because you have the best of teachers, you have the space to do it, and you have the facilities. And in terms of putting down time, the priority for someone in prison, I presume, is to get out of it as soon as possible and to spend the time as productively as possible, and to that end education provides you with a very positive way of spending your time. It certainly beats moping around and playing cards. Not that there's anything wrong with playing cards, but this provides the opportunity for people to develop talents that they may have.

One of the big things in here is, people don't have to worry about their meals or where they're going to sleep or if they've a toothache, or whatever. There are excellent services here: medical, psychological, probation, education, and so on.

But when they go outside the door there is nothing. So, one of the peculiarities of this situation, to my mind, is that you've a wonderful, a very comprehensive, service here for people who are guests of the nation, and then, when they cease to be guests of the nation, they've got nothing. They may be homeless, for example. They may have health problems. They may need to get a medical card, in which case you need to get a doctor, which is not easy these days, they tell me. So while you're here, all these things are provided and education is, you know, a good option. When you're on the outside there are other far more pressing and immediate priorities, such as the house, the dole, work, training, or whatever. And education slips down on the list of urgent and immediate things to do, which is why the local drugs taskforce established a model post-release service.

It's turned out to be incredibly useful because no statutory authority has any remit or any responsibility for people when they leave the prison. Nobody picks it up. The probation services provide a wonderful service for people in here and people before the courts, but when they are no longer subject to the direction of the courts, the probation services don't have a function.

I've seen many people go out of here and they could not recognise the city that they had left five years previously. I remember driving a guy down through Blackpool in my own car. And he just didn't know where this place was, because the flats were gone, the road had changed, there was a different configuration on the place. Like, it was, shock, horror, you know? So you can appreciate then what it must be like to go out of here being homeless, being an addict or an alcoholic, or having some difficulty in that area, and trying to get a grip on where you're going to start."

Colm O'Herlihy is Director of Education in Cork Prison.

Una O'Sullivan

"It's funny, I suppose; we kind of fancy ourselves as designers, if you like. So we try to offer people a service that is particular to them and particular to their site – if they have a site chosen by the time they come to us, which most people would.

We get all types of clients. We get the type of client who walks in here with everything set out on graph paper. They're so definite with what they want. And really and truly speaking, that kind of client will never get proper value out of us, you know? We want a client who has a good sense of what they want but is open to ideas as well. Because you can imagine if you're building a house for yourself, yes, you do have a very personal idea of what you want.

You've a very definite idea also of what you don't want and you should be walking away from us with something that addresses all your requirements physically, as regards your accommodation and everything like that. Really it should be something quite novel and something that would make you say, 'I wouldn't have come up with this in a million years myself and yet it still is my four bedrooms and my living rooms, but it's far different to what I would have come up with myself.'

I'd be the youngest of what is – nowadays – a large family, of seven. Dublin city life was never going to be for me. Sometimes maybe now I would relish the anonymity, but that definitely wasn't for me. I would just be probably more comfortable in a small community and felt we were a Bandon-based family; there's seven of us and we wouldn't be that far-flung. Bandon was just home, and particularly when I was heading for setting up something on my own, there's no question about it but that the fact that you're semi-known gives you a more ready start than you would have going in somewhere as a complete stranger. Well, particularly going into a small-town situation as a complete stranger. I suppose the few contacts I had were a bit of an asset in setting up, so that sort of copper-fastened the notion.

I wouldn't have left Dublin saying, 'I'm going to set up business in Bandon.' I would have left Dublin saying, 'I'm going to maybe get myself a job in Cork city and maybe work out of Bandon or something like that.' I suppose I then found when I was in that situation, the nature of the work I was doing, I just felt, I'd be better doing this for myself, I'd be getting a better kick out of it and more flexibility.

And, I suppose, anyone who has a bit of creativity, it's very difficult to actually get to a situation in an office where you really feel that that part of what you have to offer is being utilised, because every office has a style that they're trying to generate themselves. They'll use their architects and that, but you're very much working to that office's style or agenda. Here I'm doing it for clients, but I feel that I can pop something on the table to them and absolutely stand over it and promote it and sell it to them or whatever and tweak it and change it – ten times if necessary to get it right.

I just felt I'd get an opportunity to be a bit more creative working on my own."

Una O'Sullivan studied to be an architect in Dublin and practiced there briefly before returning to Bandon where she now has offices.

Denis O'Sullivan

"I'm not sure whether it was my dream or everybody else's dream, but everybody kept telling me, for years, 'Jesus, you should play the Senior Tour.' And there were so many people saying it to me it kind of became part of me and I started looking forward to being 50, which is very wrong. I'm not even sure that I was really dying for it, but everyone else was dying for it for me, so, I said I'd have a go. Now, I was still an amateur and the problem was, when I stood up on the first tee in France, I became a pro, which was very worrying for me because I had been an amateur from the late '60s up to the '90s, so I was an amateur 30 years.

I went to a place in Northern France to qualify. I think I was about the only amateur going. And went not having a clue what the standard was. Everybody told me I'd be wasting my time. Everybody told me I was out of my brains. They were laughing at me. I mean, all the guys who were pushing me to go were suddenly saying, 'Oh, who do you think you are?'

Yes, I'd played golf for years, but I'd played amateur golf for years. And here I was, going to try and compete with the likes of the Tony Jacklins and Tommy Hortons and Christy O'Connors, all these guys who were all my heroes down through the years. And I'm kind of thinking, 'It's an awful cheek to be doing this.' Anyway, I qualified. I got my card. And I'll never forget driving out the gate, driving home. I don't really remember the car touching the road, I was so happy; I thought I floated all the way home.

I went out then, I didn't know what to expect. I'll never forget standing up on the first tee in Spain. I thought everybody in Spain could hear my knees shake! I was petrified because I didn't know what to expect. I mean, here I was and they called me 'the amateur.' I as known as 'the amateur' to everybody for a couple of years until I won. But because I'm Irish and I'm friendly and I'm easy to get on with, I got on there with everybody. And at that stage, even though they were taking the piss out of me, I didn't care. It worked immediately – now, it wasn't big money, but I was able to pay for myself and make a few quid – and I finished ninth in the Order of Merit that year.

The only thing that saddens me a little bit about it is that this is my seventh year on tour. I can't believe it and everybody else in Cork can't believe it. When I talk to them they'll always say, 'Is this your third year on tour?' The problem is, the weeks fly. I know when you get older the weeks fly, but they really fly. I mean, we don't have a summer. We're working every day, seven days a week. We've 22 tournaments this year and I would have five or six weeks outside that of Pro-Ams and bits and pieces away in other places.

Hang on, I'm not complaining! I love it. I love what I'm doing. I really do. But I'd love to get back here. The one thing is that I miss, I miss all the friends I'd have down there. I suppose I've a lot of very good friends on tour. But they never make up for the old friends."

Golfer Denis O'Sullivan plays on the European Seniors' Tour, "the friendly tour." His partner, Paula, is his caddie.

Deirdre Ó Tuama

"I was in college and I did agricultural science. I was, I suppose, at a crossroads in my life. My father Barra was also changing direction. He'd been working in the fertiliser industry for a lot of years and he had been doing this sort of thing on a very amateur level as well. So, he decided he wanted to do this as a way to earn a living, and he asked me if I would come back and help him. I did and I'm still here, marriage and three children later!

The types of shows that we put on, they're sort of 'top of the ops'; instead on putting the full opera, we put on the well-known arias, duets, or trios from the most popular operas. We use national talent, we use local talent and we use international talent. We've been presenting four or five concerts around the country annually for 21 years. We start in September, we have concerts in November to January, then March and April, and then that's the end of our season.

The rest of the time we're mainly looking for sponsorship. Sponsors are our lifelines: we can't exist otherwise, because we're not grant-aided. We have to look for commercial sponsorship, and, so, the rest of the year is spent looking for sponsorship and looking for talent

I would say there was a great knowledge of opera among the people of the less well-off areas in Cork. Going back to the '50s and even before it, Cork used to get the travelling operas, before the days of television, the days of the spectacular cinema.
Between the old Opera House and the Savoy, a lot of opera used to come to Cork. There definitely was and is a great appreciation of opera there. What worries me a little bit is, I don't think the younger people coming up are as open to it: there are too many outside influences. Life nowadays is so fast: there are so many things happening and everything has to be fireworks and glittering lights. I suppose opera isn't regarded as being like that.

But the Italians, Bulgarians, Russians, Romanians, French always comment when they come to Cork on the absolutely fantastic tribute that they get from the people. That is one of the things that would bring them back here. People really show their appreciation and that might not be the case in a lot of other places where they perform.

Going back to the 1950s, opera was like premiership football. Back then, famous opera stars were not on the same money or the same adulation as, let's say, the likes of Pavarotti, Domingo, Cura. Starting with them, that's when opera took a turn: it became popularised, to a certain extent. Before, it was more accessible to people, whereas now, if you want to go to Covent Garden to see a performance, to see anybody of any note, you're talking about paying somewhere between £150 and £200. That doesn't make it accessible to a whole lot of people.

When Barra started this back in 1984, his idea was to bring international singers in at affordable prices. We have concerts here where people can come into the performance for €10. There isn't a huge amount you can do for €10! And we are talking about world-class calibre singers. We would go and look for talent and catch people just on the brink, before they absolutely explode. People who have performed here over the years with us have gone on to phenomenal careers. That has been our aim all the time: to make opera accessible to as many people as possible."

Deirdre Ó Tuama is Managing Director of Barra Ó Tuama Promotions Ltd. From Douglas, she now lives in in Glanmire, with husband John Healy and children Jennifer, Amy and Chloe. She loves going to opera around the world and bringing top-class opera to Irish audiences.

Youen Jacobs

"I sailed in to Baltimore, sometime at the beginning of May, I don't remember the date exactly, 35 years ago. 1969. And I was on a boat, not sailing very well upwind. When we arrived in Baltimore, we were supposed to go to Galway. But that was the beginning of the leisure boats coming up to Ireland from France; we were one of the first ones. And the wind was north north-west all the time, so we stayed in Baltimore, and when we wanted to go back to France, the wind was South East. So we stayed three weeks more. And by that time, I had decided to stay in Baltimore.

So, we were about a month here, I had phoned my boss and told him I wasn't coming back and I found a job on a fishing boat. That's how I stayed. Met my wife, fairly soon after, at the same time, and I stayed since. Myself and Finbarr Murphy, we went fishing for crab. We put our experience together on everything and succeeded to get huge amounts of crabs. We landed a ton of crab here every day.

From there, in the winter, I used to go fishing for herrings, and after that, when I came back here, I decided to start something of my own. Basically, I caught a lot of shrimp and I got somebody to put up a fish factory here, we ran it together. I was doing the fish-buying for him, and improving the fishing around the coast, giving pots to fishermen all the time, and the shrimp kept coming: for the islands, it made them. 33 years ago we bought £6000 of shrimp from the fishermen just in Baltimore, Sherkin, Hare Island, and a bit of the river. When you think that the council wages at the time were £20 a week, that was a lot of money.

The factory is still there, but we had to close after about five years. You would get a lot of bad debts in exporting fish; the money's difficult to get, and that's not a joke. You sell fish in a restaurant, people will pay straight away, after the meal. It's a better way of making money! I used have to spend days in Holland, weeks in Holland, Normandy, weeks in Brittany, weeks in the North of France, trying to get the money for fish exports. I finished with fish when a fellow left me down with £24,000 26 years ago. That was a lot. His bank was after securing the money, but the bill of exchange came unpaid, after his own bank had secured the money! You can't win in that business.

When you live in the country, you know everybody. They know you. They know you sometimes better than you know yourself. You are surrounded by people you know, sometimes your enemies, sometimes your friends. Most of them are friends. You know, in trouble, they will all come to help you, including the enemies. In cities, people are indifferent, you don't even know your next-door neighbour very often. Completely different life. You have friends but they aren't real friends: you see them coming into the pub and going out of the pub but you ignore what they do the rest of the time.

I hate cities. Even Cork I can't take. Dublin, London, Paris. Paris! I had to go to Paris before: it was a nightmare!"

Youen Jacobs hails from Brittany, and after landing there by accident in 1969, opened his first restaurant in the West Cork town of Baltimore 25 years ago. In the mid-90s, he opened another: the Jolie Brise. Now, with tongue in cheek, he boasts that he has "taken over the Waterfront," a bar-restaurant in the centre of the village.

Sheila O'Driscoll

"75%, or 80% of people here would be involved in fishing. Well, it's 100% really, because you've no farming land here: it's all too rough. Anywhere around the Beara area, there's very few able to make money off the land. So, there's someone out of every house involved in fishing. Nearly every house you go into has a husband, a father, or a son at sea, or, if not, in one of the factories. It's all rotated around fishing. If you didn't have fishing here, you could close the door from Glengarriff down.

When I got married first, in 1960, we were living down in Baltimore. My husband was from down there, and all his brothers: they're all fishing people. There was a lifeboat in Baltimore. And then we moved up to Castletown in 1967. This was a big fishing village, whereas Baltimore was not – it was more yachts; there were a few boats there, but not a lot. So, I thought we should have a lifeboat here too. And then, in Christmas 1968, there was a bad tragedy: the Seaflower was lost up Kenmare Bay with five crew. Valentia Lifeboat went up there, but it was too late. They were gone. Nobody knew whether a lifeboat would have been able to help her, mind.

It left a desperate mark on the place. If it's only one person out of the whole area is lost at sea, the whole town is in mourning. That's the size of it: Castletown is like a big family.

From then on, we kept pushing. We said we'd have to. With a big fishing port, we needed a lifeboat. We started rolling from there: fundraising, collecting, everything.

We got the boat in 1997. October '97. She was a busy boat while she was here, let me tell you: she saved a lot of lives, went out to a lot of casualties. She proved herself that we needed a boat. Even since we've got the new boat, there have been lots of call outs. They've saved a lot of lives. And they've brought in a lot of boats that were in danger or whatever. If you bring in a boat that's in danger – if there are people on the boat – you can consider that a life saved. 'Tis great security to know that if you're in trouble, they'll be out in a short time.

Our new one is here now and we're over the moon. But the people are very good; the fundraising is very good here and all over the Beara area. They're the best in the world when you go out on any kind of collection. They're very, very generous. It shows that the people of the town are concerned; they want the lifeboat, because they wouldn't give the money if they didn't appreciate what they have. And that's the backbone of it. You're depending on the people to give you the money to prove that the lifeboat is needed here. You've to prove to the RNLI, that you need a lifeboat, and the only way you can prove that is if people give money. 'Tis they put the lifeboat there and 'tis up to you to show that people appreciate it through the money you collect.

Every year then, on the first Sunday of August, there's a mass down here on the pier for the blessing of the boats. The Mná na Mara women go out with a wreath of flowers to the harbour's mouth: they go out on the lifeboat and throw it out to sea, in memory of all the people who were lost."

Sheila O'Driscoll campaigned for nearly 30 years to have a lifeboat stationed in Castletownbere, on the Beara Peninsula in West Cork. Her son, Brian, is currently the coxswain of the new Castletownbere lifeboat which was launched in 2004.

Billy Coleman

"People look at rallying and they say, 'You must need nerves of steel,' but that's actually not quite true. When you put on the helmet, you feel very secure in the car. Looking from the outside, I don't think you have to be quite the daredevil that you might seem to need to be.

The adrenaline takes over. I've gone through situations in a car at high speeds that, in the cold light of day, you'd wonder how you ever did it, or how you ever got out of a certain situation.

But, undoubtedly, in the heat of the moment, all your faculties are channelled into dealing with that situation in split seconds, and, I suppose, really, that's what makes a driver. Maybe not everyone could do that, same as I couldn't hurl to get on the Cork team. Although, I've often thought that the attributes you need to be a top hurler would often make you a very good driver: the vision you need with the speed of the ball, the eyesight, the reflexes, the balance. I met DJ Carey there some years ago – very briefly – at a race meeting up in Gowran Park and I was saying that, but I don't know whether he quite agreed! There are a number of skills that I would think are common. Mind you, I don't think you'd have to run very fast to drive a rally car!

A great friend of our family was the great Christy Ring. He used to work for Shell Oil, driving, and I used to often get a lift from him back to the city on a Monday. He was an extraordinary man. I don't think we'll ever see his equal.

If I were as single-minded as Ringy, I'd say I could have got to a considerably higher level in motorsport. He was so dedicated; you could see it in his eyes, even. He was the most intense man.

I retired in 1987. I was nearly 40 and I'd had enough of it at that stage. Nowadays, people are driving into their mid-40s and I probably could have kept going for a number of years, but I really felt I'd done enough.

Some of the enjoyment was gone out of it at that stage. It had become extremely competitive and you were expected to perform. I had my farm at home, which I was more interested in at that time and I just decided to call it a day, really. After 17 or 18 years, mind; I'd a fairly long career.

I always had the farm. My mother was from a farming background, all my uncles were in farming, so, really, from the time I could walk, I was on farms. My interests were two-pronged I suppose: farming and rallying. There was frequently a conflict of interest: I often had to leave busy seasons of the year to go away on rallies.

It was difficult: the time you might be away might be the time that coincides with good weather. It's not like a job where you can split up your work into bundles, go away and do it later on. With farming, it could be raining for two weeks and suddenly, when it's time to go, the weather could clear. And farming is entirely dependent on that! I probably never achieved my best in the sport because of that. I was never really single-minded enough. At the level I got to, you needed to be doing nothing else, and I wasn't entirely happy with that situation; that was one of the main reasons I got out of it."

Billy Coleman was Ireland's most successful ever rally driver. His career spanned almost 20 years until he retired in 1987. Born in 1948, he lives in Castlemagner, County Cork. His father owned a garage in Millstreet, which helped nurture Billy's interest in cars. He won the Circuit of Ireland three times and the Cork '20' rally six times, as well as major rallys in the UK and Europe.

197

Sadr Aziz

"I left Iraq because of my political activity and my working life and my ideas.

I ended up in Ireland. I didn't decide to come to Ireland. There was no plan when I left home that, 'My destination will be Cork.' I never knew that there was a city called Cork. I heard of Ireland before, especially Joyce – he is translated in Arabic and Kurdish and Persian – but it was never my intention to come to the country called Ireland and live here. I ended up here!

Obviously when you leave the border of Iraq, then you think, 'Now I have no home anymore. Now I'm out of home so I have to find somewhere else.' When I was in Iraq I would have liked to live in a country like Canada, but I couldn't do it. So I end up in Ireland. Probably because it's halfway!

It was September 1999 when I came here. I spent the first three months in Youghal. But you can't live in Youghal, especially if you are foreign: it's a very small size!

I had to leave. I wanted to study and then, two weeks before the millennium, I came to Cork. I stayed in Gardiners Hill for almost all the time, with a nice family. They sold the house three months ago. Now I am moved to the South of Cork. I still miss North!

There, I was living in St. Luke's. I never had any trouble. It was nice – quiet, clean, good people. Still I go back to the butcher there to buy the best meat! I think the circle I live in, people are friendly. I don't have problems with them. I'm not going to venture too far in other places, anything like that. So I meet somebody through somebody else. So no, I haven't had any problem with racism here, but that doesn't mean there's no problem.

At the start, it was not difficult, but challenging, especially because you can't reach the others. You have no language. You don't know how to express yourself, how to do anything. And you have no choice. You have to learn and you have to work hard and it's not easy, especially if you start from scratch. And if you have ambition to study, also, there's a different level of language. You can have a just speaking level, or just learning language through communication. It's different to learning to read or write or doing bloody exams! I did it! I managed. I ended up even working on a radio station!

At the very beginning when I came to Cork, I did beginner, if not elementary, English. And then I went up the levels until I did my Cambridge exam. I needed that to get to college, so I had to start studying. It's difficult, English. It's totally different, everything: writing, grammar, way of expression. You have to move everything from your personality. You have to think in a different way. You have to express yourself in a different way. You are entering a new world of idiom and expression. Totally different. It's a difficult experience but it's a nice experience. Now, when I learn English, I feel like the doors have opened and it gives fresh access to information and a lot of things. It's like building a bridge with every aspect of life.

I like Cork, but there's something in my blood that I always like not to decide to stay forever. There is a certain 'nomadity' that is part of my identity. A little bit of a traveller!"

Sadr Aziz is a Kurdish political refugee. He is currently studying in UCC. He works as a translator and is also a volunteer with Cork Campus Radio.

Trish Edelstein

"I'd always felt that somehow, living in Cork was never going to be a permanent thing; it was always going to be something that was temporary. Then Sean died eight years ago and it was just extraordinary: all these people from Cork who I'd just seen on the street and the sudden sense of support from them was extraordinary. I suppose that was when my relationship with Cork changed and I felt that, 'Maybe I am part of Cork.'

I didn't think about it before that, perhaps because of my background. I was born in France, my father was a German Jew, so his family moved from Germany to France just before the war. My mother lived in Ireland, and then she moved to France, where she met my father, and then she worked in the States, and I then moved from different parts of Ireland and England. So there was always this sense of movement. And also a sense of displacement: my father was Jewish, my mother was Church of Ireland, but my grandmother was Quaker. There was a real mixture of different religious influences on my life. So I think that, 'Where do I belong?' question has always been with me.

I work in a lot of different parts of Europe and I've brought a lot of groups here to Cork, so I seem constantly, at least two times a year, to be bringing people to Cork and showing them Cork. So there is that sense of pride when people are admiring the market, or admiring the architecture of the city. They feel like they're in a little Venice sometimes: that's often been said to me. I think always that when I'm in Cork and when I'm showing them around Cork, it's like seeing it with a new eye. Even along the Lough, at certain times of the year, watching the cherry blossom, it's wonderful. I think it's a very pretty city.

I'm gradually beginning to feel that, maybe, Cork is my home. But then, I was in Italy on my holidays and I was thinking, 'Mmmmm, maybe it's time to move on again!' I'm quite a restless person…20 years is a good stretch of time to be somewhere.

I like the humour here as well. It has a sardonic edge to it, but I like that. I think that I'm very interested in language, and there's the way Cork people never say, 'No,' they say, 'I will, yeah.' Those kind of things I like. For someone else coming in, they wouldn't understand that at all, but that's something I would have been quite interested in: the structure of language and how you go from one area to another and how it changes. If anyone has a love of a language, Ireland is a really interesting place to come to, for that reason alone, because so much of its speech is influenced by the Irish language. It flows beautifully. Compared to listening to English people speaking, it's so different.

I live in Cork, but through my work, I look out. Maybe that's why I've been able to stay in Cork for so long! I don't feel it's one foot in, one foot out, but it makes it manageable for me. I think it's more about me than Cork though.

My children love Cork as well, they've gone to university here and they think it's home. And there's a familiarity, even with people whom you don't stop and say hello to, there's a recognition there. It's like a small village really."

Trish Edelstein first came to live in Cobh 20 years ago. Her theatre company, Boomerang, was formed 10 years ago, and works with young people and youth groups in Cork, Ireland and all over Europe. She also founded the YOUCAN North-South arts' network.

Jim D'Arcy

"If we're brewing Beamish, you should be able to smell it coming down Barrack Street. Stout brewing is different because you have roast barley, which is black, almost burnt barley, and you use a different yeast too. Stout is not treated like a lager; it's not filtered as such, because you don't need it to be totally bright: it's a dark product. The nice presentation – head and all that – is produced by adding in nitrogen at the kegging stage, so it's not as gassy as other beer, but it presents a lovely creamy head. Stout is much more of a drink than lagers: there's more to it. Smoothness, fullness, maltiness, the whole lot. It's a more satisfying drink. Well, I think: it depends on what you're used to, I suppose.

In the brewery here, we have this famous 'Quarter-to-One' panel The tasting is a religion in here: the daily taste panel. It would vary from five to seven members. No, there are no vacancies at the moment! But any junior brewer here, they're all encouraged to take part and learn the trade as they go along.

The beer is tasted before it's packaged, and it's tasted again post-packaging: we just make sure that it's within this very tight band of flavour profile before going out of this brewery. A lot of bigger breweries don't get to that detail of tasting every batch, but we do, we have this daily taste panel, whereby we taste each batch. We go through the panel and pick off the various attributes. Occasionally, once a year maybe, you might come across a batch that something has gone wrong with: you might have to blend that, destroy it, or whatever.

It's mainly a sip-test, because you could have as many as 20 samples around the table. And, if you were actually swallowing a lot of that, your tasting ability would go downhill. And we have to work afternoons as well, like! It works very well. Because we're a very small brewery, we're very careful of our products going out the door – we want to make sure they're 100%.

The Brewers' Bar is where we do our taste panel. We get a keg off our kegging line and we pour it in there, or if we get a complaint keg back from the trade, it would go in and we'd test it. There's always some fresh beer and some kegs from the trade. We would have the odd other taste panel at five o'clock, tasting some kegs that we'd sent out over the previous five weeks, just to see how their shelf-life was progressing.

Then there is the after work bit. Occasionally, the taste panel goes out and we do a trade survey, where we might visit five or six pubs and taste our product, to make sure it's OK. All pubs are different: they have different type of coldrooms, different pipeline layouts, and the product might be in the keg for longer. So, that's why you get variations between the various pubs in terms of the individual product.

The thing with stout is that it has to present a nice, white head; otherwise, people won't drink it. It's very much drinking with your eyes: there's a mystique about it, settling and all that. Black stout with no head? Nobody would drink it. It's a big part of Irish pub life too: 40% of it is stout. And there's Beamish in nearly every pub in Cork, so it's part of the culture here. It's our native product, Beamish; it's here since time began."

Jim D'Arcy is Head Brewer at Beamish and Crawford. From Bansha, County Tipperary, he lives in Glanmire with his wife Maria and children Kathy, June and Seamus. He is Chairman of Sarsfield's Hurling Club.

Mary O'Driscoll

"We were founded in 1996 and we're co-sponsored by Northside Community Enterprises and FÁS. We are officially a training programme for FÁS and we are an employment project within Northside Community Enterprises. And the most important sponsor, in terms of making it happen in the first place, is UCC: the Department of Folklore and Ethnology/Béaloideas. They were the people that gave us the impetus to do it; they wanted to create what is still a unique project: we're community-based, but with academic connections and support, so that our archive and our collecting is all supported by that Department. Everything is up to correct official archival standards, in the way we index everything and that sort of stuff. If something happened to us, our entire collection could fit exactly into what UCC is doing; so, it's all very academically correct.

The ideal also was to create a community, urban-based folklore project, because so many people, when they think of folklore, think of old folks by the fire in the country! But folklore is alive and living and is everywhere: it's in the city as well as in the country. It was, originally, aimed specifically at Northside culture, because there is such a strong persona and character and community there, but it's become much broader than that now. Northside, as a name, now more refers to where we are located than what we focus on, because our focus is all of Cork. We do features in our magazine about Northside and Southside and out in the county. The collecting is the primary thing: recording interviews, recording video footage and then taking photographs and storing all of those as a resource for the community. So, we are open to anyone who wants to come in, unlike many archives that are in academic settings, where you have to show your PhD, or show that you're a student in that university – whatever - to get in. Anyone can come in here, listen to our recordings, see our photographs, make use of the archive. It could be somebody that's just interested, for their own purposes. We've had researchers as young as 12 or 13 that are working on school projects.

Our magazine, 'The Archive,' comes out once a year, and we made a very conscious decision at the beginning that this was to be a free magazine; that the material comes from the community, so we would give the magazine back to the community for free. Which means that the big problem coming up to that time every year is, the money! It is quite expensive. We do all the labour and create the material: no one's paid for any articles, so it's all printing costs. But it costs about a euro a copy to print. So, it gets pricey.

Some people go, 'What's an American doing in that job?!' But I'm an administrator: I'm a project manager. All the researchers, all the people who do the work on the project, almost all of them, are from Cork: we have one Kerryman, but he's been in Cork for about 10 years. I'm here through a grant through UCC, but everyone else who's on the project is on a CE scheme or a Job Initiative scheme. Basically, they're people from the community.

Considering that we were founded only in 1996, we have a very high profile. In fact, the Heritage Council holds us up as an example to other organisations and other groups in Ireland, as a model of what can be done. We're proud of what we've achieved in the few years we've been around."

Originally from Minnesota, USA, Mary O'Driscoll is the Project Manager of the Northside Folklore Project, located in Sunbeam Industrial Estate in Blackpool. She moved to Ireland with her husband to lead a quieter life.

Dr Tony O'Brien

"Marymount has served the people of this region for a long number of years. Its history goes back to the Sisters of Charity, the Irish Sisters of Charity who established a hospital on this site going back to 1870. I suppose, more recently, the work of the hospice has become more developed and more refined. It focuses primarily on the care of patients with advanced disease and it focuses not just on the individual patient but very much on the patient in the context of their family, because it's recognised that, if an individual within a family is ill, that has profound implications for the wider group, young and old. Everybody who might be close to that person will be affected. So, very much at the core of hospice philosophy is the view that the family is the unit of care.

Primarily, we would want to focus on achieving good pain control: making sure that people are comfortable; that they don't suffer unnecessarily from any troublesome symptoms and pain or anything else. And having achieved that then, I suppose, very often, people will want to look at some of the bigger issues that are impacting on their life at that time and look at ways in which they can address them. And this could be personal issues, interpersonal issues, business issues, legal issues, spiritual issues.

One of the philosophies of hospice care is that the care goes to wherever the patient needs to be or wishes to be. So, whilst from the perspective of the public in Cork, the word 'hospice' might be used to describe the building here on Wellington Road, in fact, the philosophy of the hospice goes way beyond this building, such that the vast bulk of our work is conducted in people's own homes, where teams of healthcare professionals from the hospice here would visit patients; wherever a person might be during the course of a serious illness, they can engage there with hospice care. So, from the patient's point of view, our primary focus is to create an environment whereby they can optimise their quality of life.

From the family's point of view, I suppose we have a similar objective, but it might be better expressed in terms of reducing bereavement morbidity because, for all of us, loss is inevitable. It's a universal human experience. We all experience loss as we go through life. That can't be avoided. Nevertheless, we realise that the level of support that people experience whilst they're going through loss can have a huge impact on their ability to cope with that loss. So it's very much a family-focused activity. And when I use the term family, I mean all those who are significant in the life of the individual patient, as determined by the patient. And that includes the youngest child to the oldest person: there are no age limitations or barriers.

It's a very challenging job. And it's also a hugely rewarding job. It's rewarding because you have, each day, an opportunity to work with and engage with patients and families at a very special time in their lives. And the opportunity to witness the capacity of the human spirit to absolutely triumph in the face of what others might regard as overwhelming adversity is really the most humbling and the most inspiring of experiences. I never cease to be amazed at the ability of individuals to face life's adversities and to address them and to ensure that even though their body might be weakened by the effects of progressive disease, that the spirit continues to grow and to mature and, ultimately, the word I would use is, triumph: the spirit triumphs."

Dr Tony O'Brien is Medical Director of the Marymount Hospice.

Fiona Kearney

"There are a couple of university galleries in Ireland but there's no university gallery that really looks to the academic community for inspiration to try and foster interdisciplinary discussions between art practice and what's happening in the university. And yet if you look at the really major established international art organisations, like MOMA or the Tate, or Pompidou...like, they had this wonderful series recently in the Centre Pompidou.

It was called 'Cloné ou pas Cloné' and it was looking at various scientific debates, but using art works and using this idea of the reproduction of art works and reproduction through various techniques and the idea of the original to raise these very serious questions about cloning. They brought in artists with scientists; an extraordinarily successful way of bringing people from the scientific community in to look at art and bringing people from an artistic community to look at science and have these discussions. I have a feeling that there's a great potential for that kind of institution and that kind of discourse to happen in Ireland that's not happening now. So, there's a very natural gap that the Glucksman Gallery can fill.

And so, for instance, for our opening displays, we have an exhibition of the work of Albrecht Dürer, who's a renowned engraver. He's one of the few artists, I think, whose name means something to everybody; there are very few artists who have that kind of impact. The show that we are doing is going to have an impact on scholarly appreciation of Dürer. But also, we'd be working very hard to produce text panels and supports and lectures that will accompany our exhibition programme, so that for someone who's completely uninitiated, either in the visual arts or in the work of a German renaissance engraver, they will have some point of engagement with the show. For the scholar who knows, say, conceivably everything there is to know about Albrecht Dürer, she or he might be surprised when they come into our gallery as well, because this would be offering them a new perspective on something that they knew profoundly well. And that's our aim.

You do both by producing the exhibitions at the highest level and then making sure that you are finding these points of engagement for every audience that you have. For instance, with the Dürer show, you could have, 'What is a print?' Just asking people to think about what is a print. For artists or people who study the history of art, they know what a print is, that's not going to be the point of engagement for them, but for someone who knows nothing about visual art, it could be really fascinating to learn about the whole engraving process and understand how a print is made.

One of the things I'm most passionate about is where this gallery is situated: behind the main gates; on a river; beside a bridge. So it has all the metaphors going for it! We're going to develop a very good schools' programme. We're doing two things. One of them is just getting them in to the gallery and getting them to think about it: that's the immediate experience. And then feeling that they have an ownership of that kind of space. If you haven't come into university before, those gates can be quite intimidating, but the gallery is saying to anybody, 'Come in.' And then hopefully further down the line we'll have kids and when they're making choices about further education, they'll go, 'Yeah, I know what that is because I've been going to the Glucksman for the last ten years.'"

Fiona Kearney is the director of the Lewis Glucksman Gallery in University College Cork.

Claire Lovett

"A day in the life could be anything from spending a day watching the delivery of bins to the halting site, to maybe being down in the Lord Mayor's Office, asking him to come on board with some idea or another, or maybe I'm at a VEC Adult Education meeting, endeavouring to provide local people with all the opportunities they deserve to further their education. Or it could be that I'm in someone's kitchen, with them at a very low point in their lives. Listening is the skill that is most required. Very often, that's all it takes to make a difference to somebody that's hurting. I treat everyone the same. Whoever you are, whatever your role is, if you are a significant adult in the child's life, I have as much business with you as with the mother and father.

My father was a teacher. We grew up in a small village outside Clonmel: he was the headmaster. I never considered doing anything else but teaching. Daddy was a teacher, my sister was a teacher; it only dawned on me 20 years later that there were other occupations out there.

I was in the classroom for 18 years, and having raised my own children at that point, I just felt that I needed to diversify a little bit. Teaching in Knocknaheeney can be challenging. Not is, but can be. All the various social issues, we see the fall out from that in the classroom.

Infrastructure is very poor in Knocknaheeney. We await the rolling out of the City Council's long-awaited 'Master Plan.'

Where many people rely on two feet or a public bus service, it is vital that services be brought to them. There's still no dental service up there. There is one doctor's surgery located in the area. No speech, psychiatric, psychological services within easy reach. There's still no bank. There's still no playground. There are still travellers living in appalling conditions. There are still some houses which aren't heated. The services aren't there. There's just a handful of shops and a pub. And when the schools close down, there's very, very little for children to do. The addition of recent Health Board projects like 'Springboard' and 'Health Action Zone' is fantastic and the completion of the new Family Centre complex will be wonderful. However, the primary school must constantly beg for monies to provide even the basics. Having to do without because of lack of money is a concept that teachers and principals have become accustomed to. This angers me greatly.

I'd have a very low tolerance now for 'petty' complaints. There is a huge divide in this city between the haves and the have-nots. Not just in the city, but all over. It is broadening all the time. To expect someone with five kids to live on €202 a week? I don't know how they do it. I think they're absolutely marvellous.

Many people in middle-class areas don't think about what it might be like to live on the breadline, or to have a drug scene going on next door, or to be depending on a local authority to come and fix things, to not have a holiday even once a year. It wouldn't even dawn on us that people have to endure the kind of hardships that people in areas like Knocknaheeney have to. The things we take for granted: clubs, classes, grinds, sports facilities…in affluent areas, it's taken for granted that children will have access to these. For many people I work with, something like music classes would be a luxury. They're a long way down the priority list. On top of that list is 'survival.'"

Having previously spent 18 years as a teacher, Claire Lovett works as a home-school liaison officer in St Mary's on the Hill National School, Knocknaheeney. Her work is focused on encouraging parents to participate actively in their children's education, and includes the provision of adult education courses and crèche facilities to members of the settled and traveller communities.

Bill Power

"Elizabeth Bowen's description is that Mitchelstown is 'a farmers' town.' It's rural, it's country-based, it's small. I would always say that Mitchelstown is too small to be a town and too big to be a village.

I'm not writing for myself, or even the people who are reading it now, but I'm putting something on record for 100 years. I'm more concerned about what people will think in 100 years: will they see it as being fair, correct, right? If you were to write for people now, to suit and to humour them, you wouldn't write at all.

Two things have influenced Mitchelstown more than anything else. One is of this idea of it being a farmers' town and the other is that it has always been a landlord town. Past and present. I've written at other times in the past that, in 1922, when Mitchelstown Castle was burned, all that happened was that the Co-op took over when the Kingstons – the landlords – left. The Co-op – the farmers – became the new landlords. They were quite conscious of this. And their big act of triumphalism was to build a massive milk-powder processing plant on the site of Mitchelstown Castle, which was the biggest house in Ireland. Obviously, things have moved on, but it's still a one-horse town in the sense that Dairygold is still the dominant force here and is likely to be for a long time to come.

If you were to ask me to define Mitchelstown historically, I would say it's regarded as one of the best-planned towns in Ireland. Arthur Young's description of it in 1777 was that, 'If you stood at the top of Galtee Mountain and looked down over Mitchelstown , the town has the situation of a capital.'

I used always say about Mitchelstown that we were about 20 minutes behind Greenwich Mean Time. So, maybe because we're that bit behind, when we do get there, we get there a little better. It's a funny one; you see the mistakes somewhere else.

At the moment, you don't see the diversity you would in other towns in terms of skin colour. It's there alright – you've Eastern Europeans – Lithuanians, Latvians – and you've Brazilians working in the meat factory. Maybe it's because there's not enough of them, but there certainly isn't any tension there. Which wouldn't be the case in other societies. It's a more subtle adjustment that's taking place here.

Mitchelstown is a bit introverted. I'm not from a farming background and one of the things I've noticed is, with farmers, because they spend so much time working on their own farm, that sort of interaction with other farms and other farmers around isn't there.

We sometimes forget that we are as good as other towns around and that we can do better than other towns around. Sometimes, you've to realise that maybe what the other fella has isn't what you want. Maybe you can do it better than he can; it isn't about keeping up with the Joneses. We should do what's good for Mitchelstown .

Mitchelstown is a kind of a frontier town as well. Within a mile of where we're sitting, there are two other counties. We could just as easily have ended up in Tipperary or Limerick, depending on what way the river flowed. So, there's all those funny interactions going on: the frontier town, the introverted town, the town that picks up on things a little slower than others, but when we pick up, we do it better than others. Somebody will probably have to write a thesis on it."

Bill Power works in heritage tourism. He has written a number of books on the history of Mitchelstown, the eighth of which was published in late 2004.

Dave Roche

"I do see now how horrendously negative it was, looking back on it from another aspect. The fact that homosexuality was still illegal, police raids on the pubs and clubs. Verbal and physical abuse – even though I didn't get much physical abuse – was quite commonplace. We had a herd mentality, so we could laugh it off in the group, but some of that does cause damage.

I suppose we would've considered it common to have people roaring at you in the street, to be calling you names. One or two of the boys got physically attacked. We accepted that as part of our lot; now, I would see that as completely unacceptable. But, at the time, that was part of being gay in this country: there was no protection, no legislation, it was still an offence in Ireland. And it was all 'underground,' in the sense that the word 'gay' itself was never spoken.

But I had quite fond memories of it myself. Now, looking back, I am aware there was another group working very strongly for political change. We had no awareness of that at 16 and 17: we were into parties and all that!

There were different layers, there were always layers in the community. We would have been very openly, quite publicly gay: we dressed in a kind of uniform, we went to all the parties and everyone knew we were gay. But behind that, there were hidden layers, from the completely closeted straight man, to the married man, to the people who wanted to interact with the gay scene but didn't want to be involved in it politically. Certainly, you didn't have the visibility that you have now.

Cork is now host to four dedicated gay outlets. That's an awful lot for a city of its size. And there are a number of other establishments that we'd class as gay-friendly. The changes now are visibility and understanding, because we always had a commercial scene.

Loafers was 20 years old this year and we had Hills and Slicks too in the '80s. Hills used to have a disco on a Sunday morning! I have fond memories of that, but I suppose the energy we put into our social lives was nervous energy: we modified our behaviour in every other sphere of our lives: at home, at work, even on the streets. You had to modify your behaviour: you couldn't relax; you couldn't act the way you wanted. I couldn't walk down the road holding my friend's hand or my lover's hand. All of that part of life had to happen undercover, behind a protective wall and that is another major change. A lot of that is now much more visible around the city: people aren't afraid to show their affection, or to be physically out. Before, it used to be more of a political statement. Of course, I wasn't sophisticated enough to know that; I was naive at the time but the extrovert side of my nature was some subconscious hope; an obvious way to make a statement about being out and drag other people with me. In a way, I suppose the change over the years has forced me to go back in. That sort of visibility is not required any more: the level has changed.

There was a fear of rejection for gay men, so we would steer away from certain pursuits and activities and socialising, either because we thought we were being barred or we were being barred. Now, those barriers are breaking down. Not broken down completely, but I hope that most gay men will realise now there is very little they can't do. That's the message we're here to try and get across."

Dave Roche is the Community Development Manager with the Cork Gay Community Project. Originally from Kanturk, he moved to Cork with his parents when he was eight, and came out at the age of 14, in the 1980s.

The Other Place
Community Development Project
Tel: 4278470
Web: www.gayprojectcork.com

Sheila O'Flynn

"Nowadays, compared with 1984, you do a real good, elaborate brochure. And, of course, marketing has come such a long way: we used photocopy a photograph onto the brochures in 1984. Now, everything is technology-driven. You get your photographs and you do a floor plan and you make up a really nice fancy brochure – not hugely costly, of course, when you think about it – you organise your sign and you put it on the market and it's just constant feedback then. At the end of the day you're employed by the vendor to get the best price. And that's where I see my role, being in there in the middle: to get the purchaser to buy it and get the vendor to sell it and just being all above board.

The role hasn't changed over the years. Literally, an auctioneer's role 20, 30 years ago was the same as it is today. Most of our sales in Cork would be done private treaty, as distinct from maybe auctions in Dublin; Cork auction properties wouldn't work the same way as they would in other parts of the country. We'd be mainly private treaty: you give as close a guide price to the selling as you can and then you'd be open to offers. And from there on you'd encourage bids and you'd build on the price from there.

I've never yet seen property as being a bad investment. At the worst you hold it and you rent it or you just don't sell it. But from 1984 to now, life has just been absolutely tremendous. Property has always been and will always be the biggest investment engine in my book. I've never actually seen it come down in Cork. At worst it levelled or it didn't go up.

I remember we were selling those big houses in Mount Prospect when they came on the market first. And they were £100,000. If you were selling those in the morning, they must be up around the €700,000 mark, which is six-fold. It has never stopped really.

Dublin mainly would be an auction area. Auctions in Cork have never really been as popular. I suppose everybody knows everybody in Cork, so if I take a property to auction, literally half the room will know one another and they'll be intimidated: 'So and so is here – he's more money than me'! Private treaty is better for the vendor because the vendor can know everything on who's bidding: there are no secrets in any part of the file.

Sometimes you'd bring a property to private auction if it was exceeding its price, just to secure the sale for the vendor so that someone wouldn't wake up afterwards and say, 'I'm sorry I went that price: I've changed my mind.' But really, Cork people are quite happy once they trust you. That's the biggest thing in our business. Once you've trust you'll rarely get a person looking to go to auction. They're quite happy if they know you and they feel everything is above board. That's the only way I'll operate. And there's never any squeamishness about, 'Who's the other person?' or, 'What's the bid?' You'd never get that asked now anymore. I would, maybe before, get, 'Who am I bidding against?' or 'How many bidders?' but once you've trust, really, that's your name and reputation; if you don't have that there's no point in coming into it."

Sheila O'Flynn is Managing Director of Sherry Fitzgerald's Cork office. She began work as an estate agent with Irish and European before, in 1984, becoming a founder member of Burton, Crowley, O'Flynn, which was bought by Sherry Fitzgerald in 2000.

Catriona Chambers

"My accent has been described as a mixture of Northern Ireland and of Cork. I was born in Rostrevor, County Down and I've been living in Cork for over nine years, which is why I have a mixed kind of an accent.

I live right in the middle of the city. I think it's a nice contrast because I grew up in the countryside, beside the sea. I absolutely love living in the middle of the city. I love the buzz and all the action: you're never short of somewhere to go or something to do. I thrive on the business of the city centre. I ended up in Cork and I'm delighted that I did. And I certainly feel at home here. I wouldn't be thinking of leaving at any time soon.

I've noticed an incredible change in Cork in the nine years. When I first got here, I felt it was more closed, certainly. When I went along to an audition at one point – and I have an ear for accents and I pick them up very easily – for a play that's set in Chicago, and went to adopt the accent for reading at the audition, I was told by the person who was going to be directing it, 'I don't think you'd be suitable because you wouldn't be able to do an accent.' Simply because I wasn't speaking to him in a Cork accent when I went in. He assumed that I just couldn't do anything else. Simply because I wasn't from Cork. Which actually took me back a lot. I found that an incredible attitude to have. I proved him wrong. I'm delighted I did.

I think that was the first realisation for me that it was going to take a while for me to feel accepted. I certainly felt after that, when I went into shops, I was almost afraid to open my mouth and talk. And I tried to put on a middle-of-the-road accent. As time went on I probably started to lose more of the Northern accent and adopt a bit more of the Cork accent!

Now I didn't know, there were probably a lot of other people in the city who weren't from the city, but I certainly felt very alone and it took me at least a year to settle in properly. I did feel when I first got here initially that there was an element of, how will we say, not really suspicious but just not exactly welcoming either, you know? I'm not picking on Cork people: it's the same everywhere you go. If you're not from somewhere, it's going to take a while for people to accept you as who you are and see you're not so bad after all. But it does take a little while for that to happen.

Nowadays, nine years on, people are much more open. There's more of a tolerance there to accept people who weren't necessarily born in the city. Attitudes have definitely changed. They have. I can see that. There are so many diverse cultures now. I mean, nine years ago when I had just moved here, I remember when a black person would walk down the street. And people would just stop and stare at them! As if they were a complete and utter strange being from another planet! Nowadays, people aren't batting an eyelid because it's quite normal, which is great. The city has become more diverse and more cultural, which reflects very well on the original inhabitants of the city: they are becoming more welcoming."

Catriona Chambers is the Station Manager of Cork Campus Radio 97.4FM at University College Cork. She also works for RTE Radio, and the Irish Academy of Public Relations.

Fergie Sutherland

"In training horses, you've got to know what you're doing. There are two things about it, really: the first is to know what to do; and the second thing is to do it.

It's a seriously good place to train horses, out here. That's why we have had so much success. No pollution and no distractions. Working up here on this wonderful springy turf three times a morning...the horses knew what to do with their feet by the time they'd had a few months of it. I had very good lads working with me too: I wouldn't tolerate second-raters.

We used to work the horses out on the hill behind because of the lovely ground. There's a great pull; when you're going slightly up a hill, there's no strain on the horse's forelegs and you don't have to go so fast. You get the horses fit because you let the hill do it; what we call resistance training. They came up here three times every morning, and they were pretty fit at the end of it.

We used to have two and a half horses to each man. So, they rode out twice – or, at the most, three times - and the horses were able to get plenty of time out of the stable. None of this business of a conveyer belt: training them on the horse walker, whipping them off, and galloping up a hill every twenty-five minutes. I wouldn't describe that as 'training horses.' No, they were individually handled here. I'm very firm about that: they have to get out for long enough, horses. Mine were mostly ridden out for just under two hours everyday. The success of the system was proved by the consistency with which they ran; none of this business of running a good race one day and blowing up the next: they went on and proved it.

When I was a young boy, I was very keen on hunting and show jumping and riding cross-country. Then, when I left the army I wanted a job with the horses and got a job with a very good flat race trainer, an Irishman called Geoffrey Brooke at Newmarket. I worked for him for five years and then I trained on my own.

I rode a lot myself, but not racing: I was too big for that. But I was a good horseman and I wanted to train horses and I thought this – my mother owned it – would be the ideal place to do it. It was only going to get sold otherwise. I considered it be the ideal place to train jumpers. You've got a good hill there and quiet roads: everything I wanted.

I never felt like a stranger in a strange land because there's a great free masonry among horsemen. I'm just an ordinary horseman and that's why I fitted in, because I understood the horsey people and they understood me. So I never felt like a stranger. I might have done if I wasn't involved in horses, but horses are my life. That made it very straightforward. Horses are a great common denominator anyway, all over the world. We recognise each other, horsey people.

I'm 73 now, so it's about time now I had a bit of a rest. I shoot a bit: a lot of snipe and rabbits, occasionally pheasant and occasionally duck. We're very keen on working our dogs. I still keep involved with horses. I don't keep horses in the yard, but I look after the interests in one or two horses. Try and guide them in the right direction, you know?"

The retired horse trainer, Fergie Sutherland, lives with his wife in Killinardrish, between Carrigadrohid and Macroom.

He trained Imperial Call to victory in the Cheltenham Gold Cup in 1996.

Acknowledgments

Thanks, first and foremost, to **my friends** and **parents**, for their total support while I was working on this book.

Also thanks to the Evening Echo management team of **Maurice Gubbins**, **Dan Linehan**, **Orla Keane**, **Diarmuid O'Donovan** and **Vincent Kelly** who gave me the opportunity to write this book and the back up they gave me throughout the project. Orla in particular was the driver of this project and her enthusiasm and professionalism made the concept a reality. The support team at the Evening Echo of **Barry Woods** who proofread the transcripts, **Brian Lougheed** who took the photographs of Richard Mills and I and the willing team of typists who transcribed the tapes – **Sarah Gubbins**, **Lisa Bowden**, **Kristel Cotter**, **Annmarie Fowler** and **Edel O'Mahony**.

Special mention to **Edward Butt**, graphic artist Irish Examiner, who designed and laid out the book and to **Richard Mills** who took the magnificent photographs and to his partner **Jo Kerrigan** for her support and understanding. The attitude and professionalism of Eddie and Richard made working on this book a joy. Also to **Michael Courtney and staff at City Print** for their flexibility and professionalism in printing the book.

This book would not have been possible with the access to the wonderful people who agreed to sit down to be interviewed and photographed. Each has a unique story to tell and they gave unselfishly of their time.

If I've forgotten anyone, I apologise sincerely.

Paul Daly

Index